The Ultimate Guide
OCEAN

Miles
Kelly

First published in 2016 by
Miles Kelly Publishing Ltd

Harding's Barn, Bardfield End Green,
Thaxted, Essex, CM6 3PX, UK

Copyright © Miles Kelly Publishing Ltd 2016

2 4 6 8 10 9 7 5 3 1

Authors John Farndon, Barbara Taylor

Publishing Director Belinda Gallagher

Creative Director Jo Brewer

Editorial Director Rosie Neave

Senior Editor Claire Philip

Cover Designer Simon Lee

Design Manager Simon Lee

Senior Designer Rob Hale

Image Manager Liberty Newton

Indexer Marie Lorimer

Production Elizabeth Collins,
Caroline Kelly

Reprographics Stephan Davis,
Jennifer Cozens, Thom Allaway

ISBN 978-1-78209-991-8

Printed in China

British Library Cataloguing-in-Publication Data
A catalogue record for this book is available
from the British Library

Made with paper from a sustainable forest

www.mileskelly.net

ACKNOWLEDGEMENTS

The publishers would like to thank
Stuart Jackson-Carter for the cover artwork

All other artworks are from the Miles Kelly
Artwork Bank

The publishers would like to thank the following
sources for the use of their photographs:

Key: t = top, b = bottom, c = centre, l = left,
r = right, m = main

Book:

Corbis 53(tl) Jacques Pavlovsky/Sygma;
61(br) Tui De Roy/Minden Pictures

iStockphoto.com 12(bl); 35(bl) 270770l;
57 PARETO

Fotolia.com 20(br) cbpix; 34(tr) SLDigi;
35(tr) Natursports; 39(br) Fabrice BEAUCHENE;
38(bl) Andrew_Howe; 53 icholakov; 54 ABUELO
RAMIRO; 57(br)

Photoshot 4(bl) Oceans-Image/Photoshot

Rex Features 62(bl) Bob Shanley/REX/
Shutterstock

Science Photo Library 60(tr) Walter Myers

Shutterstock.com back cover (tl) Targn
Pleiades, (cl) Ricardo Canino, (tr) Stephen Rees,
(cr) Adrian Kaye; panel background;
(rt) IM_photo; 1 Rich Carey; 2 Vilainecrevette;
3(t) Rich Carey, (bl) Rich Carey, (br) Mike
Price; 6(c) Steve Allen; 8(bl) dibrova;
11(tr) Andrey Armyagov; 13(c) Sarah Fields
Photography, (bl) Marc Witte; 14(tr) EcoView;
15(tr) Levent Konuk; 18(tl) Ethan Daniels,
(bl) John A. Anderson; 19(tr) ILeysen,
(br) Amanda Nicholls; 20(tr) Adam Ke;
21(br) Vlad61; 22(bl) Pawe? Borówka;
27(b) Krzysztof Odziomek; 31(br) Dray van
Beeck; 36(tr) BMJ, (b) Maciej Olszewski;
37(br) JeremyRichards; 39(tl) Attila JANDI;
42(br) Marcos Amend; 45(tr) Kent Ellington;
46(tr) Joanne Weston; 51(b) Christopher
Meder; 52(tr) Blaine Image, (br) Kristina
Vackova; 55(br) Jaochainoi; 56(br) tlorna;
58(tl) Arndale, (bl) aquapix; 59(tr) Ethan
Daniels; 62(tl) Vladimir Melnik

Acetate feature pages:

Hermit crab 16(tr) Jonathan Blair/Corbis,
(hl) Roy Waller/NHPA/Photoshot,
(br) Marevision Marevision/Photolibrary;
acetate (m) Photolibrary, (cl) Olga
Khoroshunova/Fotolia, (b) Mark Bowler/
NHPA/Photoshot; 2(m) Photolibrary,
(tl) Osaka Japan/Fotolia, (bl) D P Wilson/FLPA

Lemon shark 24(tr) Jeffrey L. Rotman/
Corbis; acetate (m) James Watt/Photolibrary,
(br) Simon Parker/Fotolia; 25(bl) Doug
Perrine/NPL, (br) Jeremy Stafford-Deitsch/
NHPA/Photoshot

Green turtle 32(tr) Chris Newbert/FLPA;
acetate (m) Tommy Schultz/Fotolia, (bl) Tunis
Marsh/Fotolia, (cb) Mitsuaki Iwago/FLPA,
(br) Mitsuaki Iwago/FLPA; 33(tr) Stephan
Kerkhofs/Fotolia, (bl) Mitsuaki Iwago/Minden
Pictures/FLPA, (bc) Jason Edwards/Getty,
(br) Matthew Oldfield/SPL

King penguin 40(m) Paul Souders/
Photolibrary, (tc) David Madison/Photolibrary,
(br) Yva Momatiuk & John Eastcott/Minden
Pictures/FLPA; acetate (m) DLILLC/Corbis,
(bl) Eksele/Fotolia, (cb)Tersina Shieh/Fotolia,
(br) Hiroya Minakuchi/FLPA; 41(tl) Paul A.
Souders/Corbis, (bl) James Hager-Robert
Harding/Rex, (br) Kwest/Fotolia

Killer whale 48(c) Theo Allofs/Corbis;
acetate (m) Photolibrary, (br) Jerome
Moreaux/Fotolia; 49(bl) Amos Nachoum/
Corbis

Ocean Depths Poster:

Amphipod Jeffrey L. Rotman/Corbis; Basket
star Roberto Rinaldi/NPL; Dumbo octopus
David Shale/NPL; Fangtooth fish Norbert Wu/
Corbis; Foraminifera D P Wilson/FLPA; Hatchet
fish Paulo de Oliviera/PhotoLibrary; Ray Ian
Scott/Fotolia; Sea spider Edwin Mickleburgh/
Ardea; Snipe eel David Shale/NPL; Tuna
Tommy Schultz; Vampire squid Steve Downer/
Ardea; Venus's flower-basket sponge Pat
Morris/Ardea

All other photographs are from: Corel,
digitalSTOCK, digitalvision, dreamstime.com,
Fotolia.com, iStock/Getty, PhotoDisc,
Shutterstock.com

Every effort has been made to acknowledge
the source and copyright holder of each
picture.

Miles Kelly Publishing apologizes for any
unintentional errors or omissions.

Contents

OCEANS OF THE WORLD

INVERTEBRATES

A world of water

● **Water covers** over 360 million sq km of the Earth's surface. It has been divided into five major ocean basins.

● **The five basins** are the Pacific, Atlantic, Indian, Arctic and Antarctic (Southern) oceans. The Arctic Ocean surrounds the North Pole and is largely frozen.

● **The Pacific Ocean** is 166 million sq km, it is twice the size of the Atlantic Ocean.

● **The average depth** of the Pacific is more than 4000 m, making it the world's deepest ocean.

● **With an area** of over 73 million sq km, the Indian Ocean is bounded by Asia, Africa and Oceania.

● **The Arctic Ocean**, at 14 million sq km, is both the smallest and shallowest ocean. The deepest point in the Arctic Ocean is only 5450 m.

DID YOU KNOW?

The Earth's oceans cover an area nine times that of Earth's Moon.

● **Seas are smaller than oceans** and are usually close to, or surrounded by, land. There are about 100 seas in the world. The largest are the South China Sea, the Caribbean Sea and the Mediterranean Sea.

● **The Southern Ocean** has the longest ocean current, the Antarctic circumpolar current, which is 21,000 km long and constantly moves east around Antarctica.

▼ *Oceans cover about 70 percent of the Earth's surface.*

ARCTIC OCEAN

ATLANTIC OCEAN

PACIFIC OCEAN

PACIFIC OCEAN

INDIAN OCEAN

SOUTHERN OCEAN

Studying the oceans

● **The study of oceans** and their ecosystems is called oceanography.

● **Oceanography comprises** marine geology, physical oceanography, chemical oceanography, marine biology and meteorological oceanography.

▼ *Fish biologists on a fish survey in Tabuaeran (Fanning) Island, Kiribati in the Pacific Ocean.*

● **Marine geology** is the study of tectonic plates. Marine geologists involved in offshore oil exploration and drilling also study how sediments and minerals are formed.

● **Physical oceanography** is the study of physical processes such as currents, temperature and tides.

● **Chemical oceanography** is the study of chemicals in the oceans.

● **Marine biology** is the study of ocean life – about 80 percent of the planet's life is found in the oceans.

● **Meteorological oceanography** is the study of atmospheric reactions above the oceans and the influence of the oceans on global weather.

● **Less than** ten percent of the oceans have been explored.

● **In 1960**, the bathyscaphe ('deep boat') Trieste reached the deepest part of the oceans, some 10,900 m beneath the surface of the Pacific, in the Mariana Trench. It took four hours and 48 minutes to reach the ocean floor.

Arctic Ocean

● **The Arctic Ocean** surrounds the North Pole. Unlike the South Pole, there is no landmass around the North Pole.

● **The maximum depth** of the Arctic Ocean is 5450 m but the average depth is about 1000 m.

● **The Arctic Ocean** is partly frozen throughout the year. At least half the ice melts in summer and large chunks, called icebergs, break off and float away.

● **About two percent** of the water leaving the Arctic Ocean does so in the form of icebergs.

● **The water** in the Arctic may be freezing cold, but it is still home to a huge variety of marine life. Whales, sharks, jellyfish, squid, seals, polar bears and seabirds can be found living in and around this ocean.

● **An underwater ridge**, the Lomonosov Ridge, some 1750 km long, divides the Arctic basin in two – the Eurasian and the Amerasian basins.

● **The Arctic Ocean** is linked to the Atlantic Ocean via the Greenland Sea, a narrow, deep-water gap between Greenland and Svalbard. It is linked to the Pacific Ocean via the Bering Straits.

● **The landmasses** of Europe, North America and Greenland almost completely surround the Arctic Ocean.

● **The coastline** of the Arctic Ocean stretches for some 45,390 km.

● **The Arctic** is the least salty of all the five oceans, because of all the freshwater from rivers and streams that flow into it, and the low rate of water evaporation due to the extreme cold. It also has limited connections to other saltier oceans.

▼ *Polar bears are powerful predators, and hunt for seals beneath the ice covering the Arctic Ocean.*

Southern Ocean

● **In 2000**, the Southern Ocean was officially confirmed as the world's fourth-largest ocean by the International Hydrographic Organization (IHO). It has a total area of some 20.3 million sq km.

● **The waters of the Southern Ocean** encircle the Antarctic continent, which surrounds the South Pole.

● **The Southern Ocean** extends from the coast of Antarctica to 60 degrees south latitude, where it merges with the Atlantic, Pacific and Indian oceans.

▼ *Penguins catch fish in the cold waters of the Southern Ocean and breed on the Antarctic continent and islands.*

● **The typical depth** of the Southern Ocean is between 4000 and 5000 m. The greatest depth is 7235 m, which is at the bottom of the Sandwich Trench.

● **The Southern Ocean** formed about 30 million years ago, when South America moved away from Antarctica. It has the strongest average winds on Earth.

● **The water temperature** in the Southern Ocean varies from −2°C to 10°C.

● **The area of the Southern Ocean** covered by sea ice increases over six times in winter, from 2.6 million sq km to 18.8 million sq km.

Icebergs

● **In winter**, seawater close to land can become frozen. The ice melts in summer and huge chunks, called icebergs, break off the ends of ice sheets, ice shelves and glaciers and float into the sea.

● **The process by which icebergs** break away from ice on land and move into the ocean is called calving.

● **Icebergs float** because ice is lighter, or less dense, than water. However 85 to 90 percent of the iceberg is below the water level.

● **The smallest icebergs** are called growlers. They are less than one metre high and less than 5 m long.

● **The largest icebergs** are over 75 m high and over 213 m long. The tallest known iceberg was the height of a 55 storey building.

● **The largest iceberg** ever recorded broke off from the Ross Ice Shelf in Antarctica in 2000. It had an area of 11,000 sq km.

● **The word 'iceberg'** comes from the Dutch word *igsberg*, which means 'ice mountain'.

● **When an iceberg melts**, tiny air bubbles trapped in the ice make a fizzing sound. These air bubbles also reflect the light, giving the iceberg a dazzling look and sometimes unusual colours, such as bright blue.

● **In April 1912**, the luxury cruise ship *Titanic* sank after hitting an iceberg, which probably came from a glacier in Greenland. Over 1500 passengers and crew members lost their lives in the disaster.

● **In 1987**, a huge flat-topped Antarctic iceberg, 155 km long and 230 m thick, was estimated to contain enough water to provide everyone on Earth with two glasses of water daily for about 2000 years.

▶ *Icebergs are carved into ice sculptures by the wind and the waves and change shape as they gradually drift into warmer waters and melt.*

▲ *Titanic struck a small iceberg, and within three hours had sunk in the freezing waters off the coast of Canada.*

Pacific Ocean

- **The Pacific covers an area** of 166 million sq km, approximately – about 15 times the size of the USA.

- **Larger than the total land area** of the world, the Pacific Ocean contains some 724 million cubic km of water. That is more than twice as much water as the Atlantic Ocean.

- **More than 80 percent** of the world's active volcanoes are found in the Pacific. They encircle the ocean along the continent margins to form the 'Ring of Fire'.

- **The average depth** of the Pacific Ocean is 4280 m, but the Mariana Trench and the Tonga Trench reach depths of over 10.5 km – more than twice the average depth of the ocean.

- **One hundred million years ago**, the Pacific Ocean was much larger than it is today. It has been decreasing in size as the Atlantic and Indian oceans have been increasing in size.

- **The name Pacific means** 'peaceful' because European explorers thought that this ocean had a gentler climate than the others.

- **The Pacific Ocean** contains many thousands of islands, including Japan, Taiwan, Borneo, New Guinea, Tahiti, Easter Island and the Galápagos Islands.

- **The North Equatorial current** of the Pacific Ocean is the longest westerly current in the world. It runs for 14,484 km from Panama to the Philippines.

- **A warm water current** called El Niño flows at regular intervals off the coast of Peru in the South Pacific Ocean, causing rainstorms and floods in Central and South America and bad weather in Asia.

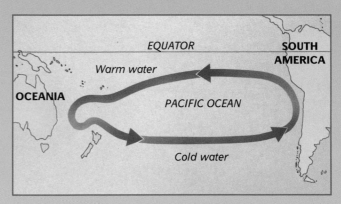

▲ Winds and the shapes of the continents make currents on the surface of the oceans flow in great circles, called gyres. The gyre in the South Pacific Ocean is one of three in the Southern Hemisphere.

▼ The Great Barrier Reef is a huge coral reef off the coast of northeastern Australia in the warm waters of the Pacific Ocean.

DID YOU KNOW?

The Great Barrier Reef is longer than the west coast of the USA. It is the largest living structure on Earth.

Atlantic Ocean

● **The Atlantic Ocean** is about half the size of the Pacific Ocean.

● **Its average depth** is 3330 m, but the deepest point is the South Sandwich Trench, which is 9144 m beneath the surface.

● **The Atlantic** is expanding at a rate of about 1–2 cm per year.

● **The floor** of the Atlantic Ocean is divided in two by an underwater mountain range, which extends from north of Iceland down to the edge of the Southern Ocean. These mountains are twice as wide as the Andes Mountains of South America.

● **Most of the Atlantic's mountains** are beneath the waves but the Azores, Ascension Island and Tristan da Cunha are the tops of some of these mountains.

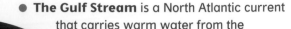

● **The Gulf Stream** is a North Atlantic current that carries warm water from the Caribbean and the Gulf of Mexico up the east coast of North America to western Europe, keeping the climate of western Europe warmer than it would otherwise be.

● **The Atlantic Ocean** receives water from about half the world's land area, including many of the world's great rivers, such as the Amazon.

● **Formed about** 150 million years ago, the Atlantic is the youngest of the world's oceans.

● **The Atlantic** is named after the legendary island of Atlantis.

▲ *In the North Atlantic Ocean, warm water circulates round and round, flowing westwards from Africa to Central America and eastwards (as the Gulf Stream) from North America to Europe.*

Indian Ocean

● **The Indian Ocean** covers about 20 percent of the global ocean between Africa, Asia, Australia and Antarctica, and is nearly eight times the size of the USA.

● **The average depth** of the Indian Ocean is 3890 m but its deepest point is the Java Trench, which is 7450 m.

▼ *One feature of the Indian Ocean is coral islands, such as the Seychelles. The beautiful beaches are popular tourist destinations.*

● **Two of the world's largest rivers**, the Indus and the Ganges-Brahmaputra, flow into the Indian Ocean, depositing fans of sediment where they enter the ocean.

● **The surface** of the Indian Ocean is dominated by monsoon winds, which blow in opposite directions during the monsoon seasons.

● **During the northeast monsoon**, the surface waters are driven away from India and towards the African coast.

● **During the southwest monsoon**, the surface waters of the Indian Ocean are driven back towards India again.

● **The floor** of the Indian Ocean is divided by a mid-ocean ridge of undersea mountains, which form an upside-down Y shape.

● **The subcontinent** of India divides the northern Indian Ocean into two, with the Arabian Sea to the west and the Bay of Bengal to the east.

● **In December 2004**, a huge tsunami in the Indian Ocean caused massive waves and flooding that devastated 11 countries and killed 283,000 people.

Ocean floor

- **The surface of the land** under the oceans is called the ocean floor. Its landscape is varied with mountain ranges, valleys, deep canyons and wide, flat plains.

- **The ocean floor** is divided into the continental shelf, the continental slope and the deep ocean floor.

- **The continental shelf** is an underwater extension of the coast. The outer rim of islands and continents gently slope into the surrounding water to form it.

- **This area contains** large deposits of petroleum, natural gas and minerals. It receives the most sunlight.

- **The continental slope** is the point where the shelf starts to plunge towards the ocean floor. The ocean floor is marked by deep canyons.

- **Below continental slopes**, sediments often collect to form gentle slopes called continental rise.

- **In many places** the ocean floor forms vast expanses that are flat and covered with sediment. These regions are called abyssal plains.

- **Abyssal plains** are broken by mid-ocean ridges, such as the Mid-Atlantic and the East Pacific rise, and trenches such as the Mariana Trench in the Pacific.

▼ *Underwater ocean features include (1) Continental shelf, (2) Abyssal plain, (3) Guyot, (4) Seamount, (5) Mid-ocean ridges, (6) Deep-sea trench, (7) Continental slope.*

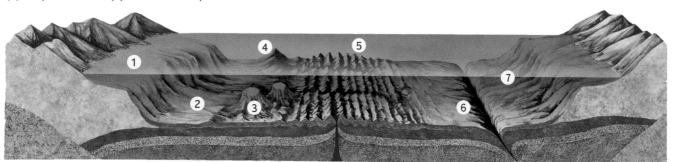

Trenches and ridges

- **Ocean floor structures** include trenches (similar to valleys) and ridges (similar to mountain chains).

- **The Earth's crust** is made up of huge rock segments (tectonic plates) that move against each other.

- **Ridges and trenches** are formed by the movement of these plates.

- **The Mariana Trench** is one of the deepest trenches. It is in the Pacific Ocean.

- **Challenger Deep**, in the Mariana Trench, is the deepest point in the Earth – it is 11,033 m deep.

- **The mid-ocean ridge** in the Atlantic is the longest mountain chain on Earth, at over 50,000 km long. The crests of these mountains lie nearly 2500 m below the ocean surface.

- **Sometimes the mid-ocean ridge** rises above the sea level. Iceland is located on a crest of the mid-Atlantic ocean ridge.

- **Seamounts are underwater** volcanoes. A flat topped seamount is known as a guyot (see above), while those with peaks are known as seapeaks.

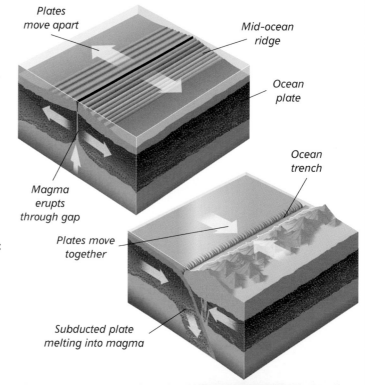

Plates move apart

Mid-ocean ridge

Ocean plate

Magma erupts through gap

Ocean trench

Plates move together

Subducted plate melting into magma

DID YOU KNOW?
The Hawaiian Islands are a chain of seamounts.

▶ *Ridges form when two plates drift apart and hot magma oozes through the cracks and cools.*

Hydrothermal vents

● **Hot springs** (hydrothermal vents) are also found on the sea floor along the mid-ocean ridge. They are formed when water seeps into the crust as two plates pull apart. This water is heated by the magma and shoots up through cracks in the ocean floor.

● **The water temperature** in and around a vent can reach 400°C. It is rich in minerals and the gas hydrogen sulphide.

● **The scalding water** mixes with the surrounding cold water to create jets of warm water. These are often black because of the mineral content in the water, so they are also called black smokers.

● **Hydrothermal vents** were first discovered in 1977 near the Galápagos Islands, along the eastern Pacific Ocean basin.

● **Some vents** form chimneys as minerals in the vent fluid are deposited around the jets of water. These chimneys can be over 60 m high and grow as fast as 30 cm a day.

● **Vents may last** from 100 to perhaps as long as 100,000 years, although they are probably destroyed sooner than this as the Earth's tectonic plates move and volcanoes erupt under the sea.

● **The water** at the deep-ocean floor is too cold for creatures to survive, but hydrothermal vents are like underwater oases. Long tube worms and other life forms that are not found anywhere else in the world thrive near these vents.

● **Vent communities** feed on bacteria, which use the minerals from the vents (especially sulphur) to make food. This is very different from most food chains, which depend on the Sun's energy to make food, and may provide clues to the scientific origin of life on Earth.

● **Giant tube worms** that live around deep-sea vents can be over 2 m long. They do not have a mouth or digestive system, but absorb food directly from the billions of microscopic bacteria living inside them.

● **An unusual worm**, called the Pompeii worm, lives right inside some of the growing vent chimneys, surviving temperatures as high as 80°C.

DID YOU KNOW?

Godzilla, a vent chimney in the Pacific Ocean, reached the height of a 15-storey building before it toppled over. It is now growing upwards again.

▼ Giant tube worms breathe through red gills, which emerge from the top of their tubes. Rattail fish use their fleshy barbels to detect small creatures in the black water.

1 Cloud of hot water rich in minerals
2 Rocky chimney made from a build up of minerals
3 Rattail fish
4 Giant tube worms
5 Giant clams

Islands

- **An island** is an area of land that is surrounded by water. Rising sea levels can create islands by cutting off a piece of land from the mainland.

- **The world's four largest** islands are Greenland, New Guinea, Borneo and Madagascar. Unique wildlife, such as lemurs, evolved on Madagascar after it broke away from the African mainland some 165 million years ago.

- **The island of Surtsey** was created by the eruption of Sutur, an underwater volcano near Iceland, which erupted for four months, from 1964–1965.

- **The 16 Galápagos Islands** are the tops of volcanoes that rose from the ocean floor and have never been connected to the mainland. The oldest islands are probably no more than five million years old and some are still forming.

- **The Maldives**, in the Indian Ocean, are made up of 1190 coral reef islands that have grown on top of an underwater mountain chain.

- **An atoll** is a coral reef surrounding a lagoon. The formation of atolls can take millions of years.

▲ *Only 200 of the Maldive Islands are inhabited. The highest point on the islands is only 2.4 m above sea level.*

- **Atoll formation** begins with the creation of a coral reef around a volcanic island. Wind and waves erode the island and it begins to sink. The reef grows upwards to form a barrier separated from the island by a lagoon. At this stage the island is called a barrier reef island.

- **The barrier reef island** sinks until submerged. The reef around the island continues to grow upwards to form a ring around a lagoon. This is called a coral atoll.

- **Coral atolls are formed** mostly in the warm, shallow waters of the Indian and Pacific oceans.

- **Waves and wind** may deposit bits of coral and sand on top of reefs. Over time, this piles up to form low-lying islands called cays.

Volcanic islands

- **Undersea volcanoes** often lead to the formation of volcanic islands. Some form around one or two volcanic vents, others can be made up of a series of vents.

- **Volcanic activity** often occurs at the point between two tectonic plates.

- **Sometimes**, volcanoes are formed away from the plate boundaries, near fixed points of volcanic activity located beneath tectonic plates (hot spots).

- **Molten magma** from deep within the mantle forces its way through fissures (gaps) in the plate and flows out to form seamounts.

- **Over millions of years**, magma oozes out of these seamounts, which rise above the ocean surface as islands. These islands are called oceanic high islands.

- **Volcanic activity** on an island stops when it is carried away from the hot spot the tectonic plates move.

- **Then another island is created** at the hot spot. This continues until a chain of islands, such as the Hawaiian Islands, is created.

- **The hot spot** in the Pacific Ocean is currently under Big Island – the largest among the Hawaiian Islands.

- **Iceland was formed** by volcanic activity near the ocean ridge. It is the only part of the mid-oceanic ridge that emerges from the surface.

▼ (1) *Molten magma breaks through Earth's crust.* (2) *More lava is deposited on the seabed, so a cone shape builds up.* (3) *When this breaks the water's surface, a new island appears.*

Waves, tides and currents

● **Oceans are continually** rocked by movements such as waves, currents and tides.

● **Most movements** are caused by wind. Waves are created by winds blowing over the surface of the oceans.

● **The water in a wave** moves in circles. As a wave nears land it slows. The top part continues and crashes on the shore as a breaker.

● **The shape and size** of waves differ. A steep, choppy wave is one that formed near the coast, while slow, steady waves are those that formed out in the ocean.

● **The regular rise and fall** of the oceans are called tides. They are caused by the gravitational pull of the Moon. The period of high water level is called high tide and the period of low water level is called low tide.

● **An ocean current** is a mass of water moving continuously in one direction.

● **Surface currents** are caused by winds and the rotation of the Earth.

● **Underwater currents** are caused by differences in temperature and salt content.

● **When the Sun, Moon and Earth** are aligned, their combined gravities cause very high tides (spring tides). Smaller tides (neap tides) occur at times when the Moon is at a right angle to the Sun and the Earth.

▼ *High tide occurs in those areas that are closest to and farthest away from the Moon. As the Earth turns about six hours later, the water subsides and low tide occurs.*

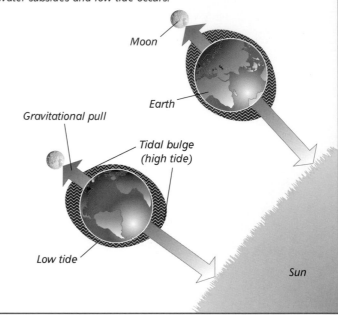

Moon

Earth

Gravitational pull

Tidal bulge (high tide)

Low tide

Sun

Danger at sea

● **The oceans** can wreak havoc in the form of tsunamis, whirlpools and hurricanes.

● **Tsunamis are massive waves** generated by certain natural disturbances. They lash against the shore with great force and can cause a lot of damage.

● **Usually created by earthquakes**, tsunamis can also be generated by landslides and undersea volcanic eruptions.

● **Most tsunamis** originate along an earthquake-prone zone known as the Ring of Fire, around the Pacific.

● **Hurricanes are cyclones** arising in tropical or sub-tropical waters. These powerful storms often travel onto land where they cause floods and devastate towns.

● **A typical hurricane** is about 500 km wide. At the centre is a small circular area with no clouds. This is called the 'eye', and it's completely calm and quiet.

● **A whirlpool is created** when opposing currents meet. Most whirlpools are not dangerous, but some are powerful enough to destroy small boats.

● **Moskstraumen** off the coast of Norway and Old Sow near Deer Island in Canada are two of the world's most powerful whirlpools.

◄ *In 2005, Hurricane Katrina flooded 80 percent of the city of New Orleans, USA. Over 1800 people lost their lives.*

DID YOU KNOW?

El Niño is a warming of surface waters in the eastern Pacific near the Equator. It can lead to flooding and drought around the world.

Coastlines

- **A coast** is a continuous stretch of land that borders an ocean. The outline of the coast is called a coastline.

- **Hard rocks** withstand the waves and erode slowly, forming headlands.

- **A cliff is formed** by the pounding of waves on weak spots on the rock face.

- **Continuous erosion** leads to the creation of hollows (sea caves). Sometimes waves pound the headland from both sides, causing two caves to form back-to-back.

- **When two caves meet**, a sea arch forms. The top of the arch links the headland to the mainland.

- **After years of erosion**, sea arches cave in and leave a sea stack – a column of rock in the sea.

- **The best known natural structure** formed by waves is the beach. Waves lose much of their power in shallow waters and instead of eroding, they deposit sand and shingle along the coast. These deposits eventually become the beach.

- **Longshore drift** is the term used to describe the movement of beach material along the shore when waves strike the beach at an angle.

- **A spit is formed** by longshore drift. It is a long, thin ridge of sand, shingle or mud, which is joined to the coast at one end but extends out into the sea. Spits often curve at the end because the waves push them back towards the coast.

- **A lagoon** is a coastal lake cut off from the sea by a bar of sand or mud (perhaps a spit joining two headlands) or a coral reef.

▼ Towering sea cliffs on the Hawaiian Islands are among the tallest in the world, and are as high as a 300-storey building.

DID YOU KNOW?

The world's tallest sea cliff is in Greenland. It is called the Thumbnail and it is nearly 1500 m high.

▼ The wind can create sand dunes on beaches, which may be covered with grass and other plants. The dunes help to protect the coastline from erosion.

Life on the seashore

● **Creatures such as periwinkles** and limpets can survive out of water for long periods at low tide. They live high up on a rocky shore.

● **Animals and plants** that need to be underwater most of the time, such as starfish, topshells and kelp seaweeds, live low down on a rocky shore.

● **The middle of a rocky** shore is underwater half the time. Animals such as barnacles and mussels survive well here, as well as seaweeds such as wracks.

● **Buried under a sandy shore** are burrowing animals such as worms and shellfish (razor shells and tellins) that feed on food particles brought in by the tide.

● **The South African plough snail** 'surfs' up the beach to feed on decaying matter and creatures stranded by the high tide. It has a muscular foot that it uses as a plough-shaped 'surf board'.

● **Rockpool fish** such as lumpsuckers and clingfish have suckers to help them stick to rocks when waves crash into their pools or the tide drains away.

● **To protect themselves** from drying out at low tide, sea anemones pull their tentacles inside their hollow bodies so they look like blobs of jelly.

● **Mudskippers** are named after their habit of 'skipping' across muddy shores by wriggling their tails. They burrow into the mud to escape danger and drying out at low tide.

● **Mangrove trees** shield tropical shores from storms and hurricanes and also build up the shoreline by trapping mud among their thick, tangled roots.

▲ *At low tide, the roots of mangrove trees look like legs supporting the trees.*

▼ *Large rockpools shelter a variety of life, from seaweeds and shellfish to starfish and crabs.*

1. *Anemone*
2. *Goby*
3. *Starfish*
4. *Hermit crab*
5. *Limpet*
6. *Mussel*
7. *Sea urchin*
8. *Sponge*
9. *Bladderwrack seaweed*
10. *Shore crab*
11. *Prawn*
12. *Topshell*
13. *Razor shell*

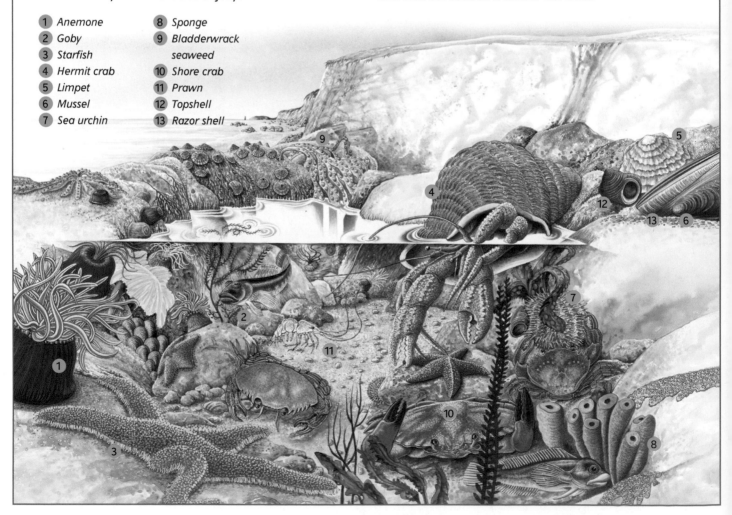

Living links

● **Ocean plants and animals** are linked by the way they feed on each other. Each plant or animal is like a link in a chain, so a series of feeding links is called a food chain.

● **Most ocean food chains** start with tiny drifting plants and animals called plankton. Plant plankton is called phytoplankton and animal plankton is called zooplankton.

● **An example** of an ocean food chain is: phytoplankton – zooplankton – mackerel – humans.

● **An example** of a seashore food chain is: seaweed – periwinkle – crab – octopus.

● **Some ocean animals** help each other to survive by living together. This is called symbiosis. Tiny green plants called algae grow on the edge of a giant clam's shell. They feed on the clam's waste and, in return, the clam feeds on some of the algae.

▲ Clown fish clean up the anemones they live with by feeding on leftover food scraps.

● **Clown fish** are protected from predators by hiding in an anemone's stinging tentacles. The clown fish covers itself in slimy mucus so it is not harmed by the poisonous stings. The bright colours of the fish may warn predators that the anemone is dangerous so that both animals are more likely to survive.

● **Cleaner wrasse fish** feed on the pests and dead skin of larger fish – they even work down a shark's throat.

● **Remora fish** are the hitch-hikers of the oceans, sticking to larger fish with a sucker on their head. When the larger fish finds food, the remora lets go and feeds on the scraps.

● **Male anglerfish** attach themselves to females because it is so difficult to find a mate in the darkness of the deep ocean. They live off the blood supply of the female and are ready to fertilize her eggs whenever she lays them.

▲ The basking shark is the world's second-largest fish, but feeds on microscopic plankton that drifts near the surface of the ocean.

DID YOU KNOW?

The banded coral shrimp cleans the needle-sharp teeth of moray eels, and gets a free meal into the bargain.

▼ Cleaner wrasse fish gather around the gills and mouth of a shark. The shark is cleaned up and the wrasse get protection and an easy meal.

Profile: Hermit crab
Borrowed home

Despite their name, hermit crabs are not closely related to true crabs. They belong to a group of invertebrates called anomurans, which have four pairs of developed legs (including the claws). True crabs have five pairs of legs including the claws.

Although they are crustaceans, hermit crabs lack an extra-hard external shell.

They have a long, soft abdomen, which they protect by hiding inside empty seashells, particularly those of sea snails. This makes these crabs seem like shy, solitary creatures living in small caves, and has provided them with their 'hermit' name.

In order to grow, hermit crabs shed, or moult, the hard covering on their bodies. They grow a new, larger body covering but this takes time to harden. Moulting makes hermit crabs vulnerable to predators as they have to wait until the moult is complete before they find a new, bigger 'borrowed' shell. Young crabs moult every few months and adults about every 18 months.

▲ SHELL FIGHTS
Hermit crabs fight over the best shells because there are often limited numbers of the right size. One crab may try to steal another's shell by evicting the owner, like this crab on the right, which lacks a shell of its own.

There are about 500 different species of hermit crab and most live in the sea. Even land hermit crabs have to return to the ocean to breed. Sea anemones sometimes live on the shells of hermit crabs and ragworms may live right inside the shell, feeding on leftover scraps of food.

▶ MOVING HOME
When they are moving into a new shell, hermit crabs are at risk from predators. They are not safe until they have squashed their strange, twisted abdomen into the coils of the snail shell.

SCAVENGER CRABS

Hermit crabs are not fussy eaters and have a varied diet. They often scavenge for rotting plant and animal remains and can also filter small food particles from the water.

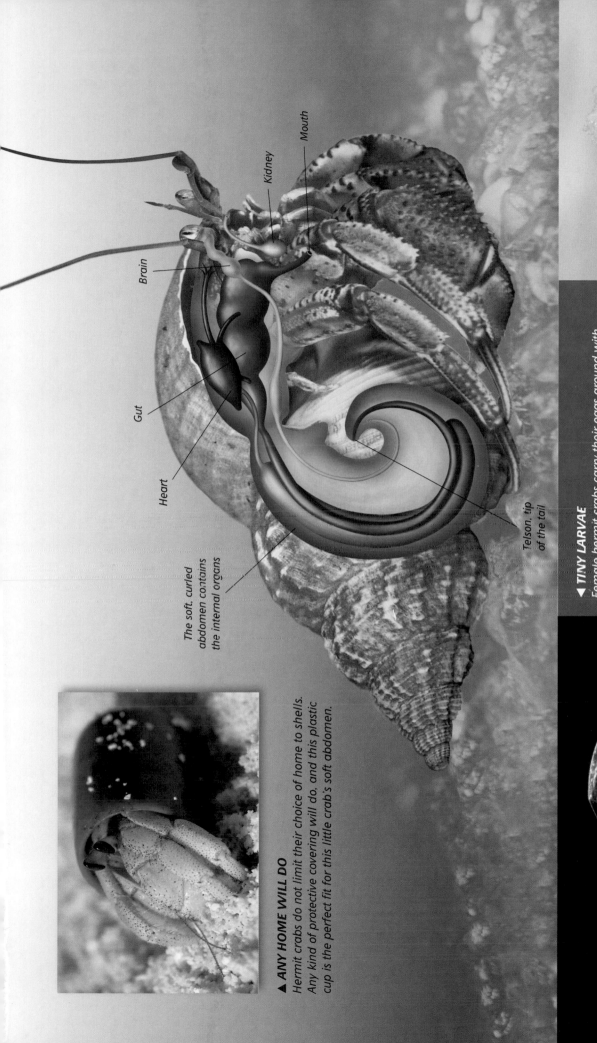

Mouth

Kidney

Brain

Gut

Heart

The soft, curled
abdomen contains
the internal organs

Telson, tip
of the tail

▲ ANY HOME WILL DO
Hermit crabs do not limit their choice of home to shells.
Any kind of protective covering will do, and this plastic
cup is the perfect fit for this little crab's soft abdomen.

◀ TINY LARVAE
Female hermit crabs carry their eggs around with
them inside their shells. When the eggs hatch, the
young go through a larval stage, which looks a bit like
a shrimp. The larvae drift in the plankton, moulting
several times as they grow and develop.

▶ FIRST HOME
After several weeks of drifting near the surface of the
sea, the larvae develop into baby crabs, which sink to
the seabed. They begin their search for small, empty
shells to use as a first home.

Crabs and other crustaceans

● **Crustaceans are named** after their hard, tough outer casings, or exoskeletons, which are made of chalky plates that cover their bodies like a crust.

● **As well as lobsters and crabs**, the crustacean group includes shrimps, prawns, krill, barnacles and sea slaters (relatives of woodlice).

● **Many crustaceans** start life as microscopic larvae that drift with the plankton, which forms the start of most ocean food chains.

▼ *A lobster uses its big claws for gripping and shredding its food. As well as its two front claws, it has eight walking legs.*

● **In the Southern Ocean**, a shrimp-like crustacean called krill is a vital source of food for many sea animals, from whales and seals to penguins and other seabirds.

● **The decorator crab** is camouflaged by seaweed, sponges and other small animals, which cover its body and are held in place by tiny hooks.

● **Goose barnacles** may drift thousands of kilometres across the oceans attached to pieces of driftwood or rafts of bubbles, which they make themselves. Most barnacles stay fixed to rocks when they are adults.

● **In autumn**, West Indian spiny lobsters migrate to the calm of deeper water to avoid storms on the coast. They march across the seabed in long lines for up to 15 km a day.

● **The Japanese spider crab** is the largest crustacean, with legs spanning 3 m. These crabs have poor balance and live in still waters, hunting slow-moving prey such as other crustaceans, starfish, worms and shellfish.

Worms

● **Ocean worms include** flatworms, ringed or segmented worms, tube-making worms, peanut worms, ribbon worms, beard worms and arrow worms.

● **Ragworms are named** after the ragged fringe of flat legs along the sides of their bodies. They use their legs for crawling, swimming and breathing.

● **The sea mouse** is a worm that is covered in bristles that look like fur. It lives on coasts near the low tide line.

● **The peacock fanworm** lives inside a tube of mud and sand, pushing a fan of feathery tentacles out of the top of the tube to breathe and catch food particles drifting past.

● **Lugworms** live in U-shaped burrows under sandy or muddy shores, swallowing the sand or mud and extracting food particles. Their waste piles up at the exit to their burrows like heaps of 'sand spaghetti'.

● **The palolo worm** of the Pacific Ocean reproduces by breaking off a special 'tail' filled with eggs and sperm, which wriggles on its own to the surface.

● **Peanut worms** are named after their shape. They have a proboscis (tubular sucking organ), which they use for feeding.

● **Giant tube worms** that live around hydrothermal vents grow up to 2 m long in the deep sea, but in shallow water, they are only as long as your hand.

◄ *Feather duster worms filter food from the water with their fan-shaped tentacles.*

Jellyfish

● **Jellyfish have inhabited** the oceans for more than 650 million years. They were living on Earth long before the dinosaurs and still survive today.

● **These creatures are not fish**, instead they belong to a group of animals called cnidarians (or coelenterates), which also includes sea anemones and corals. Most cnidarians live in the oceans.

● **A group of jellyfish** is called a smack.

● **A jellyfish** is made up of 90–95 percent water. It needs water to support its delicate body and stay alive. It will dry up and die out of water.

● **Jellyfish open and close** their umbrella-shaped 'bell' to force water out behind their bodies and push themselves along. They also drift on ocean currents.

● **Jellyfish do not have** a brain, heart, blood, head, eyes ears or bones. They can, however, detect light and dark, and scents in the water.

● **To capture prey** such as small fish, shrimps or tiny sea creatures, jellyfish use stinging cells on their tentacles. The stings inject poison to paralyze or kill prey.

▲ *A jellyfish has a bell-shaped body, which is called a medusa.*

● **The stings of some jellyfish**, such as the box jellyfish or sea wasp, are strong enough to kill a person. The box jellyfish has about 5000 stinging cells on each tentacle.

● **The world's largest jellyfish**, the Arctic lion's mane jellyfish, has tentacles up to 30 m long.

● **The Portuguese man-of-war jellyfish** has a gas-filled float, rather like a sail on an old-fashioned sailing ship. The wind blows the 'sail' across the ocean.

Sponges

● **Sponges are animals** with no brain or body parts.

● **There are about 10,000 species** of sponge. Some grow to more than one metre wide and the largest (Monoraphus) grows to about 3 m in width.

● **Most sponges** are attached to a surface. They often form a thin crust, but some are shaped like tubes, cups or fans.

● **The breadcrumb sponge** grows in flat mats over rocks. If it is touched, it crumbles into small pieces, like breadcrumbs.

● **Most sponges** have an internal skeleton made of rod- or star-shaped spicules, made from calcium carbonate or silica. This skeleton helps to support the sponge's body.

● **In the Venus's flower-basket sponge**, the spicules are fused to form a delicate, basket-like structure.

● **Bath sponges** have a very dense and elastic skeleton made of a substance called spongin. They do not have a spicule skeleton like most other sponges.

● **If part of a sponge** breaks off, it can grow into a new sponge.

▲ *Yellow tube sponges usually grow in groups, building tubes at least 60 cm high.*

● **Many sponges** give off poisonous substances to defend themselves. Some of these substances may be used by people as medicines.

● **Sponges** are filter-feeders. They strain bacteria and food particles from the water using tiny tentacles, which line chambers inside their bodies.

Starfish, sea urchins and sea cucumbers

- **There are about 7000 species of echinoderms**, which means 'spiny skinned'. They have a skeleton made of hard plates, covered by a layer of skin. In some species the plates are joined to long spines.

- **The echinoderm group** includes starfish, sea urchins, sea cucumbers, brittle stars and sand dollars.

- **All echinoderms live in the sea**, both in shallow and deep water. Their bodies are usually divided into five equal parts.

- **A starfish** has rows of tube feet underneath its arms. By pumping water into these tubes, it can crawl along. The feet are also used for feeding and breathing.

- **Many starfish** have five arms, but some have as many as 50. If one arm breaks off, starfish can generate a new one to replace it.

- **Brittle stars are relatives** of starfish, with thinner arms that break off easily if they are touched. They usually hide during the day and come out to feed at night-time.

▲ *Starfish are active predators. They can even push their stomachs out of their mouths to digest large prey that is too big to swallow.*

- **Sea cucumbers** live on the ocean floor, using a set of sticky tentacles to trap particles of food. Some can produce poisonous, sticky threads to trap predators.

- **Sea urchins** are protected by their poisonous spines. Underneath the spiny body is a mouth with five pointed teeth for scraping food from the rocks.

- **Sea lilies are echinoderms** that are fixed to the sea floor by a long stalk. Their five feathery arms collect food particles from the water.

Molluscs

- **Molluscs that live** in the oceans include a variety of shellfish (such as clams or cowries) as well as sea snails, chitons, octopuses, squid and cuttlefish.

- **Chitons have** one muscular foot and a rasping tongue (like snails and slugs) but their shell is made up of eight overlapping plates.

- **Many sea slugs** have bright colours to warn of the poisons in their bodies. Some kinds steal poisonous stinging cells from sea anemones and use them for their own defence.

- **Sea snails**, such as whelks, breathe oxygen from the water by means of gills. They draw water over their gills using a tube called a siphon.

- **Scallops are a sort of bivalve** – a mollusc with a shell made of two hinged plates, called valves. Scallops swim by 'clapping' the two halves of their shell together, forcing out a jet of water that pushes them along.

- **Pearls may grow** inside oyster shells if a piece of grit gets trapped between the shell and the thin layer lining the shell. Pearls grow at a rate of about one millimetre in five years.

▲ *Sea slugs have feathery plumes called ceratia on their backs to absorb oxygen from the water.*

- **Giant clams** can grow as large as one metre across and live for up to 100 years. The clam has rows of tiny eyes along the edge of its shell to detect danger. It heaves its shell slowly shut if danger threatens.

- **Cone shells use a tiny**, poisonous 'harpoon' to paralyze their prey, such as small fish or worms. Some cone shells can kill people.

- **Purple dye** produced from some murex shells was used to dye the cloth worn by the rich in ancient Rome.

- **Mussels produce** tough, silky threads to anchor themselves to the rocks.

Cephalopods

- **Octopuses, squid, cuttlefish and nautiluses** make up a group of molluscs called cephalopods, which have a large head, well-developed eyes and long arms with lots of suckers.

- **The nautilus** is the only cephalopod with an external shell.

- **Cuttlefish have an internal shell,** or cuttlebone, which is often washed up on the shore. The cuttlebone contains spaces filled with gas, which helps the cuttlefish to float.

- **Cephalopods swim** by jet propulsion. They squirt a jet of water out of a funnel called a siphon, which makes them shoot forwards through the water.

- **Cephalopods can change** colour almost immediately to startle predators, blend in with the background or send messages to others of their own kind.

- **The bright blue** colour of the blue-ringed octopus warns that it has a deadly bite. The rings turn blue when the octopus is threatened. A bite from this octopus can kill a person.

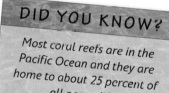

▲ *Squid are predators of fish, crustaceans and other squid. Their streamlined body shape helps them to swim fast and their long tentacles are used to catch food.*

- **The giant squid** is the largest invertebrate, with a body 2–4 m long and tentacles reaching lengths of 25 or 30 m. Its eyes are the largest of any living creature and can grow to the size of dinner plates.

- **Many cephalopods** can produce light so they glow in the darkness of the deep sea. They use their glowing lights to communicate with others or to attract prey.

- **If it is disturbed**, an octopus can shoot a cloud of murky ink called sepia into the water. This confuses the predator or sometimes has a numbing effect, giving the octopus time to escape.

- **Cephalopods** very similar to the nautilus of today swam in the oceans millions of years ago. Nowadays, the nautilus is very rare and is a kind of 'living fossil'. Its arms do not have suckers.

Coral reefs

- **Corals are ancient animals** that have been around for 400 million years.

- **Coral reefs** are formed by colonies of coral polyps – tiny animals that use minerals in the sea to produce their protective outer skeletons. These skeletons form hard and branching structures called coral reefs.

- **The polyps** use their tentacles to capture tiny creatures called zooplankton, and also eat algae.

- **Coral reefs are home** to many creatures such as starfish, reef sharks, sponges, crabs, lobsters, anemones and a huge variety of fish. The reefs are found in warm and shallow waters, usually within 30 degrees north and south of the Equator. There are three kinds of kinds of coral reef – fringing and barrier reefs, and coral atolls.

- **Fringing reefs extend** from the land into the sea. Barrier reefs are found further from the shore, separated from the mainland by a lagoon. Atolls are ring-shaped formations of coral islands around a lagoon.

- **The Great Barrier Reef** in the Coral Sea off the northeastern coast of Australia is the biggest coral reef in the world. It is over 2000 km long.

- **Reefs are also found** in the Indian Ocean and the Red Sea. Some also stretch along the Atlantic Ocean from Florida in the United States to the Caribbean Sea and Brazil.

DID YOU KNOW?
Most coral reefs are in the Pacific Ocean and they are home to about 25 percent of all ocean life.

▼ *A single coral reef may be home to as many as 3000 species of living things.*

Fish facts

- **Fish are vertebrates**, so they have a backbone. They live in water, breathe through their gills and have scales.

- **Most fish live in oceans** – only one in five lives in freshwater.

- **Fish are cold-blooded**, meaning their body temperature changes with their surroundings.

- **There are two main groups** of fish – jawed and jawless. Jawless fish, such as lampreys and hagfish, have a sucker-like mouth with horny teeth.

- **Jawed fish** are further divided into cartilaginous and bony fish. The skeletons of cartilaginous fish are made of tissue called cartilage. Sharks, rays and chimaeras are cartilaginous fish.

- **The skeletons of bony fish** are made of bone. They are the most common fish species. Most have a gas-filled swim bladder that controls buoyancy.

- **Two of the largest fish** in the oceans, the whale shark and the basking shark, feed on microscopic plankton.

- **Fish are important** to humans as food. Excessive fishing has endangered some species, while others are already extinct.

- **Some fish** of the Southern Ocean have a natural anti-freeze in their blood to keep their bodies working in freezing cold water.

- **Fish sense vibrations** caused by currents, predators and prey by means of a lateral line of nerve cells that runs along each side of the body under the skin.

▼ *Cod are active hunters, catching molluscs, crabs, starfish, worms, squid and small fish.*

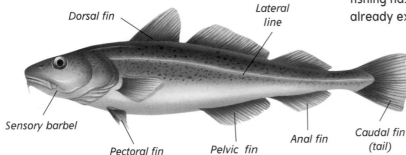

Dorsal fin

Lateral line

Sensory barbel

Pectoral fin

Pelvic fin

Anal fin

Caudal fin (tail)

Coral reef fish

- **There are more species** of fish on a coral reef than in any other place in the oceans. The Great Barrier Reef may be home to about 2000 different kinds of fish.

- **Blue tuskfish** grow up to one metre long and are strong enough to lift rocks aside with their mouths to reach crabs hiding underneath.

▼ *A variety of fish live on coral reefs because there is plenty to eat and lots of places to hide and shelter.*

- **Manta rays** are common in the waters around coral reefs. They 'fly' underwater on their huge wing-like fins. A giant manta rays weighs up to 2 tonnes.

- **If a porcupine fish** is threatened, it puffs its body up with water, making its spines stand out.

- **Surgeonfish are named** after the sharp scale at the base of the tail, which is like the sharp scalpel used by surgeons during operations.

- **Butterfly fish have long snouts** to help them to reach into small cracks and crevices in the coral to search for food. The long-snouted butterfly fish has a particularly long nose.

- **Cowfish or boxfish** are protected by bony plates in their skin, which act like a suit of armour. They also have strong 'horns' and skin poisons to keep predators away.

- **If triggerfish are chased**, they will swim into a hole and lock a spine on their back in an upright position so predators cannot pull them free.

- **Scorpionfish are well camouflaged** as they lie still among the corals, waiting for prey to pass by close enough to catch.

Seahorses

- **There are about** 35 different species of seahorse, which are named after their horse-shaped heads.

- **These fish** range from less than one centimetre to about 30 cm long.

- **Seahorses swim** by fluttering the small fin on their back, which beats up to 35 times a second. Side fins help them to steer through the water.

- **A seahorse has no teeth** and sucks up small fish, shrimps and plankton with its long, hollow jaws. It can eat up to 3000 shrimps a day. Food passes through the digestive system quickly as the seahorse has no stomach. It has to keep eating all the time to stay alive.

- **Instead of scales**, seahorses have a series of rectangular bony plates. These protect them from predators, such as crabs.

- **The female lays** up to 2000 eggs in a pouch on the male's body. The male carries the eggs until they hatch and the young are able to swim out.

- **Seahorses can change** colour to match their surroundings by expanding or contracting cells full of coloured pigment in their skin.

- **The pencil-shaped pipefish** belongs to the same family as the seahorse. It can grow to 50 cm in length.

- **The seahorse family** also includes seadragons, shrimpfish, sea moths and trumpet fish.

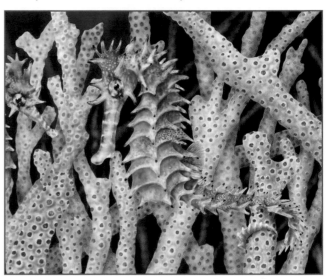

▲ Seahorses have a gripping or prehensile tail, which they wrap around corals and seaweeds. This stops them being battered by waves or washed away by currents.

Sharks and rays

- **Sharks and rays** are cartilaginous fish that belong to the same animal family. They have skeletons made of cartilage instead of bone.

- **There are over 460 species** of shark but only four regularly attack humans: the tiger, great white, bull and whitetip shark.

- **Sharks range in size** from the 23-cm pygmy shark to the 12-m whale shark, which is the world's largest fish.

- **The skin of a shark** is not covered with smooth scales like bony fish. Instead, it is covered with tiny, tooth-like structures called dermal denticles.

- **The diet of sharks** includes seals, squid, fish and other marine creatures.

- **Rays are found** in all the oceans. Most live near the seabed. They bury themselves in the sand when threatened.

- **These fish have** broad, flat bodies. Their eyes are located on the upper surface of the body, while the mouth and gills are on the lower side.

- **Rays are usually brown** or black in colour, with a light underside. Some species can change their colour to match the surroundings.

- **Some species** of ray are less than 10 cm in width, while others measure over 6 m across.

◄ Most sharks such as this Carribean reef shark have torpedo-shaped bodies and large tail fins that give them extra power. They are very efficient swimmers.

Profile: Lemon shark

Timid fish

Named after its pale, yellow-brown back, this shy shark often swims away from humans and rarely attacks unless provoked. It is usually non-aggressive towards others of its own kind. One of the larger sharks, the lemon shark reaches lengths of up to 3.5 m. Males and females are similar in size and are difficult to tell apart.

This stocky shark prefers to inhabit shallow waters, such as those around coral reefs, mangrove swamps, sheltered bays and river mouths. On migration, it swims in open ocean.

Lemon sharks feed over sandy sea floors, catching fish such as catfish, mullet, cowfish, guitarfish and stingrays, as well as crabs and crayfish. Seabirds and smaller sharks also feature in their diet.

Female lemon sharks are pregnant for 10–12 months and give birth to up to 17 pups at a time. At birth, the shark pups measure up to 65 cm in length. They are left to fend for themselves in shallow water for several years until they mature.

SAVE THE SHARKS

Lemon sharks survive well in captivity and are used in scientific research. Habitat loss and overfishing may be a threat to them. They are hunted for their meat and skins, and their fins are used to make shark fin soup.

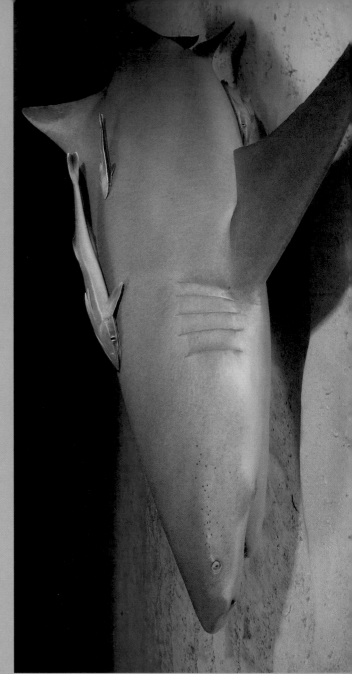

▼ NIGHT-WORKER
Lemon sharks spend the night in shallow water and then return to deeper water during the day. They are most active at dawn and dusk. This lemon shark has two remora fish attached to it, hitching a ride.

▲ FEEDING FRENZY
When a group of sharks fight for the same prey, they bite and thrash about. This is called a feeding frenzy and may be caused by stress as individuals fight for dominance.

Nasal sacs link directly to brain

Brain

Teeth are attached to the jaws by soft tissue

Skeleton is made of gristle-like cartilage, which is strong but more flexible than bone

Strong arches of cartilage support the gills

Heart

Gall bladder

Large liver filled with oil helps the shark to float

Stomach

Stiff fin filled with rods of cartilage helps the shark to balance in the water

Kidney

Intestines have a spiral valve to help with nutrient absorption

Backbone extends into tail

▲ DIVING WITH SHARKS

Lemon sharks are bigger than humans and their large size and powerful bite make them potentially dangerous to divers.

▶ BEING BORN

The pups develop inside their mother, receiving nutrients from her body by means of a yolk-sac placenta. They are born in shallow water in spring and summer.

▶ GROWING UP

Newborn pups hide in mangrove swamps where they are protected from predators such as other sharks. They will not breed until they are 6–7 years old, and may live for up to 27 years.

Incredible hunters

● **Sharks are excellent hunters** – they have keen senses that help them hunt and travel great distances.

● **Teeth are** a shark's most powerful weapon. A shark can have as many as 3000 teeth, in three rows.

● **It is thought** that almost one-third of a shark's brain is devoted to detecting smell.

DID YOU KNOW?

Some sharks have special eyelids called nictitating membranes. These close to protect the eyes from being damaged.

● **Some sharks** have whisker-like projections on their snouts (nasal barbels) to help them feel for prey.

● **Sharks also have** good eyesight. Most of them hunt at night and have enhanced night vision.

● **The ears of a shark** are inside its head. Each ear leads to a small sensory pore on the shark's head.

● **It is believed** that sharks can hear sounds over a distance of 250 m.

● **Sharks have** an extra sense organ called the lateral line. It runs down each side of the body, under the skin.

● **As a shark swims**, ripples pass over the lateral line through its skin. Tiny hairs inside sense the ripples and send signals to the shark's brain.

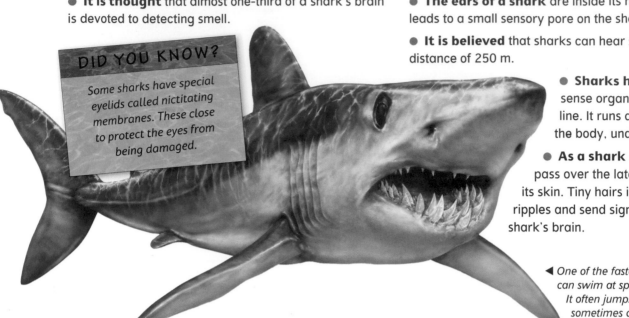

◄ *One of the fastest sharks, the mako can swim at speeds of over 48 km/h. It often jumps out of the water, sometimes as high as 6 m.*

Great white shark

● **The great white** is the largest predatory fish. It has a pointed snout and a large tail fin.

● **Commonly found** in temperate waters, great white sharks are grey in colour, with a white underbelly.

● **The great white** is normally about 4.5 m in length, but it is thought that some grow as long as 6 m.

● **The 3000 teeth** of great whites have saw-like (serrated) edges, and can grow up to 7.5 cm long.

● **This shark** hunts sea lions, seals and sea turtles. Young great whites eat fish, rays and small sharks.

● **Unlike other sharks**, the great white does not have a protective membrane to cover its eyes. When it attacks, the shark rolls its eyes back in their sockets for protection.

● **The great white** usually approaches prey from below. Sometimes it will jump out of the water. This is called breaching.

● **Without a swim bladder** to keep them afloat, great whites have to swim continuously or else they sink.

● **Female great whites** give birth to live young.

● **Unlike other sharks**, the great white does not have a protective membrane to cover its eyes. When it attacks, the shark rolls its eyes back in their sockets for protection.

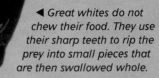

◄ *Great whites do not chew their food. They use their sharp teeth to rip the prey into small pieces that are then swallowed whole.*

Hammerhead shark

● **Hammerhead sharks** have a wide, hammer-shaped head. Their eyes are located on either side of this 'hammer'.

● **The head contains** tiny receptors that detect prey. Its unusual shape also helps the shark to take sharp turns.

● **The hammerhead is common** in tropical and temperate waters. It is grey or brown in colour, with an off-white belly. This shark migrates towards warmer waters near the Equator in winter.

● **The first dorsal fin** of the hammerhead, located on its back, is large and pointed. Like most sharks, it can be seen cutting through the surface as the shark swims.

● **The great hammerhead** is the largest member of the hammerhead family. It can reach up to 6 m in length. Bonnethead sharks are smaller and have heads shaped like shovels.

▲ *The great hammerhead is an excellent hunter. It uses its highly developed senses of smell and direction to track prey.*

● **Hammerheads feed** on fish, smaller sharks, squid and octopuses. Stingrays are their favourite food.

● **Large teeth** enable the great hammerhead to bite big chunks off its prey.

● **Other varieties of hammerhead** include the scalloped and the smooth hammerhead. Both types are found in moderately temperate waters.

● **Most hammerheads are harmless**, but the great hammerhead is one of the few dangerous species. It is known to have attacked humans.

Whale shark

● **Although they are the largest fish** in the world, whale sharks are not aggressive and pose no threat to humans.

● **Whale sharks live** in warm, tropical waters.

● **The average length** of a whale shark is about 14 m, but some have been known to grow to over 18 m long.

▼ *Grey or brown in colour with an off-white underside, the whale shark has white dots and lines on its back.*

● **An average** adult whale shark weighs about 15 tonnes. Owing to their size, these sharks cannot move fast. They swim by moving their bodies from side to side.

● **Although whale sharks** are usually solitary, they have been observed swimming in schools.

● **The mouth of the whale shark** is enormous and can be as wide as 2–3 m. It contains around 300 rows of tiny, hook-like teeth in each jaw.

● **As they swim** with their mouths open, whale sharks suck in water. Bristles on their gills filter their tiny prey, while water passes out through the gill slits.

● **The diet of whale sharks** consists mainly of plankton, sardines, krill and anchovies.

● **Whale sharks** are known to wait at fish breeding grounds to capture freshly laid eggs to eat.

Deep-sea fish

● **Over 300 species of fish** live in the deep ocean at depths below 1000 m, where they never see sunlight.

● **The greatest depth** at which a fish has been recorded is 8372 m in the Puerto Rico Trench, the boundary between the Caribbean Sea and Atlantic Ocean. This fish has been named *Abyssobrotula galatheae* but very little is known about its biology.

● **Food is hard to find** in the deep ocean so fish have to rely on fragments of food floating down from above ('marine snow') or eat other deep-sea creatures.

● **Deep-sea fish** usually have big mouths, long, sharp teeth and stretchy, expandable stomachs to help them catch as much food as possible when they do find a meal.

● **As there is no light** in the deep ocean, many fish produce their own light to help them find a mate or attract prey. This production of biological light is called bioluminescence.

● **The deep-sea anglerfish** has a 'fishing rod' growing out of its head, which glows in the dark because it contains luminous bacteria.

● **The gulper eel** has huge hinged jaws, which allow it to swallow prey much larger than itself.

● **The viperfish** is named after the long fangs that stick out from its jaws, like the fangs of snakes, called vipers. The teeth point backwards to form a cage, so that fish cannot escape once they are caught.

● **Deep-sea hatchet fish** have large, tubular eyes that point upwards to look for food falling from above. They migrate to shallower waters at night to hunt for small fish and plankton.

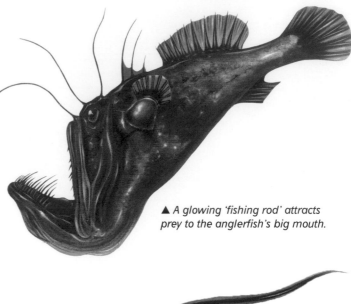

▲ *A glowing 'fishing rod' attracts prey to the anglerfish's big mouth.*

▲ *The gaping mouth and stretchy stomach of the black swallower allow it to eat fish much larger than itself.*

▲ *Hatchet fish have light organs on their body called photophores. These help with camouflage and flash on and off in a special pattern during courtship.*

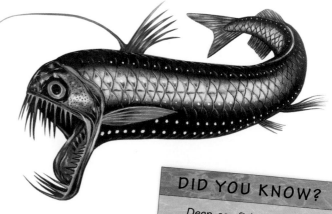

▲ *Viperfish are fierce predators of the deep sea. Their long, needle-like teeth are used to trap prey.*

DID YOU KNOW?

Deep-sea fish have soft, flabby bones and flesh to help them withstand the enormous water pressure.

Barracuda

- **Barracuda are powerful predators** – in some coastal regions, they are more feared than sharks.

- **These fish have** long heads and slender bodies. They vary from 40 cm to almost 2 m in length.

- **Powerful swimmers**, these fish are found in the tropical waters of the Pacific, Atlantic and Indian oceans.

- **The mouth contains** a number of fang-like teeth. These predators have a forked tail, and their dorsal fins are widely separated.

- **The great barracuda**, found in the Pacific and Atlantic oceans, grows to a length of 1.8 m and can weigh as much as 41 kg. Also called the 'tiger of the sea', this aggressive predator is known to attack divers and swimmers.

- **The diet of barracuda** includes sardines, anchovies, mullet, bream, grunts, groupers, snapper and squid.

- **Smaller barracuda** swim and hunt in schools, while larger ones hunt alone.

▲ *Barracuda are fearsome predators. They seize, maim and tear up other fish with their fang-like teeth.*

> ### DID YOU KNOW?
> The flesh of some barracuda species is toxic to humans because the fish they feed on are poisonous. The barracuda are immune to this poison.

- **Barracuda make** surprise attacks on their prey, relying on sudden bursts of speed to catch a meal. They can swim at speeds of up to 45 km/h.

- **Few predators** are large and fast enough to catch the great barracuda, but sharks and tuna feed on small adult barracuda.

- **There are about 25 species** of barracuda and they live for about 10–15 years.

Swordfish

- **Found in tropical** and temperate waters, swordfish are mostly dark in colour, with a lighter-coloured belly.

- **Swordfish get their name** from their upper jaw, which extends to form a long, sword-like snout with a sharp point. This jaw does not have teeth.

- **Swordfish can grow** over 4 m in length. The 'sword' accounts for almost one-third of this. The jaws of a young swordfish are equal in length. The upper jaw grows longer with age.

- **The snout is used** for both defence and attack. Swordfish probably dash into schools of fish to injure or spear their prey.

- **Mackerel**, herring and other small fish that swim in schools are the usual prey of swordfish. They may also dive deep in search of sardines.

◀ *The 'sword' of a swordfish can be up to 1.4 m long.*

- **Like marlin and sailfish**, swordfish are powerful swimmers. They swim long distances to catch prey.

- **The crescent-shaped tail** is characteristic of fast swimmers belonging to the same family. Swordfish do not have pelvic fins.

- **Swordfish can swim** at speeds of up to 100 km/h. Some gather in schools, but most are solitary.

- **Females are larger** than the males and produce tens of millions of eggs at a time. Adults live for around nine years.

Herring

- **Herring are often found** in the waters of the North Atlantic and the North Pacific oceans.

- **There are over 360 species** in the herring family, which includes sardines, anchovies and shad.

- **Sardines are named** after Sardinia, an island in the Mediterranean where the fish were once abundant.

- **Herring species vary** in size from the Baltic herring, which is 14–18 cm long, the Pacific herring, which is 38 cm long, and the Atlantic herring, which reaches about 46 cm in length.

- **Herring feed on** small fish and plankton. They are an important part of the diet of larger creatures such as sharks, seals, whales and seabirds.

- **A female herring** produces up to 40,000 eggs each year.

- **The wolf herring** is the largest of the herring family. It is a fierce hunter and can grow to one metre in length.

- **Unlike most fish**, herring have soft dorsal fins that have no spines. They also have no lateral line to sense vibrations in the water.

▶ *Herrings have streamlined bodies and usually swim in large schools.*

- **Herring are processed** and sold in several forms. They can be smoked, dried, salted or pickled. Kippers are split and smoked herrings, a bloater is a whole smoked herring and rollmops are pickled herring fillets.

Tuna and mackerel

- **Tuna and mackerel** belong to the Scombridae family of fish.

- **These fish** are fast swimmers. Their torpedo-shaped bodies and crescent tails help them thrust through the water at great speeds.

- **Mackerel** have sleek, shiny bodies and large mouths. The head does not have any scales.

- **Found in cool waters** around the northeast United States, Canada, Great Britain and Norway, mackerel remain close to the surface and eat small crabs and fish.

- **The Atlantic mackerel** is the most common variety. It is blue and silver in colour and can grow up to half a metre in length.

- **Tuna need lots of oxygen** so they swim with their mouths open, shooting jets of water over their gills. Oxygen is extracted from this water.

- **This method of breathing** means that tuna can never stop swimming.

- **Tuna are not cold-blooded**, instead their bodies keep a few degrees warmer than the water.

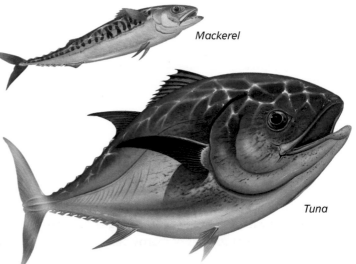

Mackerel

Tuna

▲ *A mackerel's back shows a greeny-blue sheen, but its underside is pale, allowing it to camouflage itself and surprise its prey. Tuna are more rounded and sleeker than mackerel.*

- **Schools of tuna** can travel long distances. They come to coastal areas to lay their eggs. The eggs usually hatch within 24 hours.

- **Bluefin tuna** are large marine fish. Adults weigh over 680 kg and can swim at a speed of about 90 km/h.

Flying fish

- **Flying fish** do not actually fly. They leap into the air and glide for short distances.

- **The average length** of a flying fish is around 20–30 cm. The California flying fish, found in the Pacific Ocean, is the largest species. It can grow up to 45 cm in length.

- **The pectoral fins** of flying fish have similar functions to a bird's wings. The two-winged flying fish have very large pectoral fins that they stretch out to soar.

- **Some flying fish** have four 'wings'. In addition to large pectoral fins, these species also have large pelvic fins.

- **When threatened**, flying fish build up speed under the water's surface by thrashing their tails and holding their fins close to the body. The fish then leap into the air and glide for about 45 seconds.

- **Flying fish can leap** to a height of 1.2 m and cover a distance of over 200 m. In between glides, they return to the water to gain speed.

▲ *The ability to glide helps flying fish escape from sea predators such as tuna and mackerel. But once in the air, they become the target of seabirds.*

- **These fish can glide** at double the speed they swim, and are known to accelerate from 30 km/h in water to 60 km/h in air.

- **Young flying fish** look very different from their parents. They have whiskers on their lower jaw, which disappear as they mature.

- **Usually**, flying fish swim in schools. Sometimes a whole school leaps into the air and glides together.

Eels

- **Eels are snake-like fish** that live in shallow waters. Most live in the sea, but a few are found in freshwater.

- **Most species of eel** are around one metre long. However, the conger eel can grow up to 3 m in length.

- **Eels are normally found** among coral reefs and on the ocean floor. There are about 700 eel species. The most common include the conger, moray and gulper.

- **A species of moray eel** found in the Pacific Ocean has been known to grow over 4 m in length. There are about 200 different species of moray eel.

- **Eels do not have a tail fin** as their dorsal fin, which runs along the top of the body, provides them with the power to swim.

- **Some species** have scales, but the bodies of most eels are covered with a slippery layer of mucus.

- **Eels are graceful swimmers** but are not very fast. Some species, like the American eel, can breathe through their skin and can survive for some time out of water.

- **Eels have over 100 bones** (vertebrae) in their spine, which makes their bodies very flexible.

▲ *Fan-like structures on the nose of a blue ribbon eel probably help it to sense an approaching meal.*

- **There are about 20 species** of garden eels, which live in colonies in shallow water. Their heads poke out of the seabed like walking sticks to catch food drifting past in the water. In the densest colonies, there may be as many as one eel every 50 cm.

- **Adult European eels** live in rivers but migrate to the Sargasso Sea, in the North Atlantic Ocean, to breed. Their eggs hatch into leaf-shaped larvae, which drift about the oceans for three to four years. When the larvae mature into young eels, called elvers, they swim back into the rivers until it is time for them to breed.

Profile: Green turtle
Armoured reptile

Named after the green colour of its body fat, the green turtle is protected by its tough, bony shell, which surrounds its body like a suit of armour. The flattened, streamlined shell is designed for swimming, and unlike its land relatives, the green turtle cannot pull its head and neck inside its shell.

The green turtle has extremely wide, powerful front flippers that it uses to propel itself through the water. Its rear flippers are smaller, and are used like rudders for steering and brakes for stopping. This turtle can reach swimming speeds of up to 30 km/h and can remain underwater for about 30 minutes at a time.

Female green turtles are extremely good at navigating their way through the oceans, and may travel hundreds, or even thousands, of kilometres to find a suitable nesting beach on which to lay their eggs. Very often they nest on the same beaches where they themselves hatched out. These heavy creatures find it difficult to move on land – they can weigh up to 227 kg. As soon as the females have laid their eggs, they return to the water, leaving the eggs to develop alone. Only one in 1000 baby turtles will survive to become adults.

TURTLE THREATS

Green turtles sometimes become tangled in fishing nets, and may be strangled or drowned if they cannot swim to the surface to breathe. Other threats include pollution, disturbance and degradation of nesting beaches, collection of eggs and being killed for their shells, meat or body parts.

▼ FEEDING
Mainly vegetarians, green turtles graze on the seagrass and algae that grow in warm, shallow seas. They will also eat jellyfish and sponges when they can. Turtles do not have teeth, but their sharp, jagged jaws work like garden shears to cut through their food.

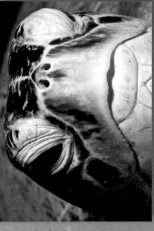

▲ GOGGLES

Green turtles have large upper eyelids to protect their eyes while swimming. They can see well underwater but cannot see long distances when on land.

▲ TURTLE RIDERS

Remora fish sometimes hitch a ride on a green turtle's shell, using a strong sucker to hold on tight. They may feed on scraps of food left over by the turtle.

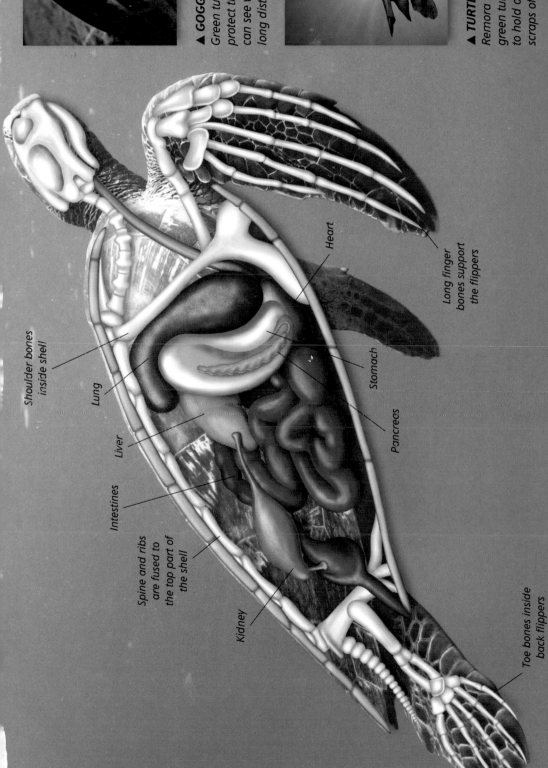

Shoulder bones
inside shell

Lung

Liver

Intestines

Spine and ribs
are fused to
the top part of
the shell

Kidney

Heart

Long finger
bones support
the flippers

Stomach

Pancreas

Toe bones inside
back flippers

◄ HATCHING OUT

It takes about two months for a baby green turtle to hatch. An egg tooth on its snout helps it to break free of its egg.

► FREE AT LAST

The tiny baby turtles work together to dig their way out of the nest. It takes them several days to struggle free of their deep sandpit. They scuttle down to the sea as fast as they can, swimming until they reach deeper water, where they are safer from predators.

The eggs are covered by soft shells and are about the size of table tennis balls.

Sea turtles

- **There are only seven species** of marine turtle. They are found in tropical and sub-tropical waters around the world.

- **The leatherback turtle** is the largest. The other species are loggerhead, hawksbill, olive ridley, Kemp's ridley, flatback and green turtle.

- **A hard shell** covers and protects all sea turtles except the leatherback. These shells are flat and streamlined to allow water to flow over them easily.

- **The shell of the leatherback** turtle is made of a thick, rubbery substance that is strengthened by small bones. This turtle is named after its unusual shell.

- **The front limbs** of sea turtles are larger than the back. These flipper-like limbs help turtles to 'fly' through the water, although moving on land is quite awkward.

- **Sea snakes and sea turtles** are the only reptiles that spend most of their lives in the ocean. Female turtles swim ashore for a few hours each year to lay eggs.

- **Females prefer to lay their** eggs at night. They dig a pit in the sand with their flippers then lay about 50–150 eggs, and cover the nest with sand.

▲ *A female green turtle covers her eggs. Green turtles are named after the colour of their body fat, which is green due to their diet.*

- **Once the eggs hatch**, the young turtles struggle out of their sandpit and make their way to the sea. On the way, many babies fall prey to seabirds, crabs, otters and other predators.

- **The diet of sea turtles** differs from species to species. Leatherbacks prefer jellyfish, while olive ridleys and loggerheads eat hard-shelled creatures such as crabs. Sponges are a favourite of hawksbills.

- **Most turtle species** are under threat because they are hunted for their eggs, meat and shells. The trade in turtles has been declared illegal in most countries, but people continue to kill them.

Sea snakes

- **Sea snakes** are commonly found in the warm waters of the Indian and Pacific oceans. Their venom is more powerful than that of most land snakes.

- **Fish**, eels and fish eggs are the preferred diet of sea snakes. They use their venom to kill prey and then swallow it whole.

- **Sea snakes are covered** in small scales. These reduce friction, helping the animal to swim faster. A flat, paddle-like tail aids swimming.

- **To breathe**, sea snakes have to come to the surface. They can stay underwater for long periods because they absorb some oxygen from the water and have an extra-large lung.

- **A gland** under the tongue helps a sea snake get rid of excess salt from seawater. It also has highly developed nostril valves that can be closed while underwater.

- **Most sea snakes** never leave the water. Females give birth to live young in the water.

- **Five species** (the sea kraits) lay eggs on land instead of giving birth to live young.

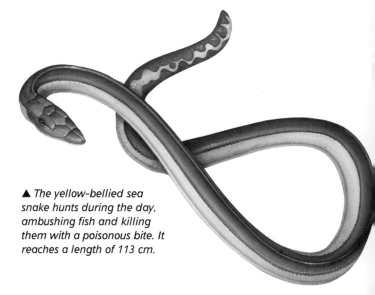

▲ *The yellow-bellied sea snake hunts during the day, ambushing fish and killing them with a poisonous bite. It reaches a length of 113 cm.*

- **Sea kraits** have coloured bands on their bodies. Unlike true sea snakes, sea kraits have wide scales on their bellies that help them to move on land.

- **The yellow-bellied sea snake**, named after its bright yellow underside, is the most recognizable true sea snake. It is poisonous, but attacks only when disturbed.

- **The fastest swimmer**, the yellow-bellied sea snake can reach a speed of 3.6 km/h. It can stay underwater for three hours before coming to the surface to breathe.

Marine iguanas

- **The marine iguana** of the Galápagos Islands in the Pacific Ocean is the only ocean-going lizard in the world.

- **These unusual lizards** live on rocks around the coasts, diving into the sea to feed on underwater algae and seaweed. Their short, blunt snouts and razor-sharp teeth help them to scrape their food off the rocks.

- **Marine iguanas** dive to depths of more than 15 m and stay underwater for up to an hour, although dives of 5–10 minutes are more common.

- **The sea around the Galápagos** is cold, so the marine iguana slows its heart rate when it dives, to stop it losing too much heat through its skin.

- **Long, sharp claws** help the marine iguanas to cling to slippery rocks on the shore, or hold onto underwater rocks in the strong currents around the Galapagos Islands.

▲ Marine iguanas bask on the rocks to warm up in the sun. Their bodies need to be warm to digest their food and their dark colour helps them to absorb heat rapidly.

DID YOU KNOW?

To get rid of excess salt, marine iguanas sneeze. The expelled salt covers their heads like a white wig.

- **Strong swimmers**, marine iguanas lash their tails from side to side to push through the water.

- **In the breeding season**, males defend groups of females against rival males.

- **Breeding males** develop colourful patches of red and green skin, which help them to attract females.

- **At night**, marine iguanas huddle together to sleep in groups. This helps them to keep warm and save energy.

Saltwater crocodiles

- **The saltwater crocodile**, or 'saltie', is the largest crocodile in the world, reaching a length of up to 7 m and weighing up to one tonne. Salties are the world's heaviest living reptiles.

- **These crocodiles live in rivers**, estuaries and oceans over a wide range, from southern India and other parts of Southeast Asia to northern Australia and the island of Fiji in the Pacific Ocean.

- **Excellent swimmers**, saltwater crocodiles have been spotted hundreds of kilometres out at sea.

DID YOU KNOW?

Saltwater crocodiles are increasingly threatened by habitat loss, pollution and illegal hunting.

- **These crocodiles** can reach swimming speeds of 24–29 km/h in short bursts, but generally cruise at 3–5 km/h. They prefer to drift in calm water near the shore rather than swimming in stormy seas.

- **Saltwater crocodiles** try to use as little energy as possible. This helps them to survive for months at a time without eating when food is scarce.

- **Compared to other crocodilians**, the saltwater crocodile has less armoured scales on its neck and back. This makes it easier for the crocodile to bend its huge body when swimming. Heavy scales would also weigh it down too much out at sea.

- **These huge crocodiles** feed on a variety of animals including fish such as sharks, turtles, birds and even mammals.

- **Saltwater crocodiles** have efficient salt glands to help get rid of the extra salt from seawater before it is absorbed into their bodies.

◀ Saltwater crocodiles warm up by basking in the sun and cool down by swimming or floating in the water.

Albatrosses

● **The three great albatrosses** – royal, wandering and Amsterdam – are the largest of all the seabirds. They weigh up to 10 kg.

● **Albatrosses live** in all oceans except the North Atlantic, but 17 out of the 22 species live only in the area covered by the Southern Ocean.

● **The wandering albatross** has the greatest wingspan of any bird, measuring about 3.4 m from one outstretched wingtip to another. That's more than three times the distance between your outstretched arms.

● **Most albatrosses** are white or pale grey in colour, with black wing tips. Some have brown feathers.

● **Albatrosses have a sharp bill** with a hooked upper jaw. They also have tubular nostrils and webbed feet. Their long, narrow wings make them powerful gliders.

● **Squid**, cuttlefish and small marine creatures are the favourite prey of albatrosses.

● **Of all seabirds**, albatrosses spend the most time at sea. They even sleep while floating on the surface of the ocean. They come ashore only to breed.

● **Albatrosses nest in colonies** on remote islands. Many have complex mating dance rituals.

● **These birds can travel** thousands of kilometres over the oceans in search of food for their chicks. The parents swallow the prey and regurgitate (cough up) the food into the chick's bill when they get back to the nest.

● **There is a superstition** among sailors that killing an albatross brings bad luck. This belief forms the theme of Samuel Taylor Coleridge's famous poem 'The Rime of the Ancient Mariner'.

◄ The black-browed albatross is named for its dark eye stripe. It has a wingspan of 2–2.4 m.

Gulls

DID YOU KNOW?
Kelp gulls steal food from penguins and also harass and rob other birds of their food.

● **Many birds** live around the oceans. The most common are gulls (seagulls), which are migratory. There are about 43 species of gull.

● **Gulls range in length** from 28–80 cm. Most have a white and grey plumage. Some have black markings on the back, wings and head.

● **The plumage** changes colour throughout the gull's life, and some have winter and summer plumage.

● **Many gulls** are great scavengers and feed on dead matter along seashores.

● **Black-headed gulls** have dark heads and red bills in summer. In winter their heads turn white with a grey spot. It is thought that this gives better camouflage.

● **Gulls are able to fish** in shallow waters and often prey on the eggs of other seabirds.

● **Some gulls nest** on ledges in cliffs. However most make simple grass-lined nests, mostly on flat ground in isolated areas on beaches.

● **A sharp, hooked bill** helps gulls to kill small birds and other prey. They have webbed feet to paddle on the water's surface, but they cannot dive underwater.

◄ This herring gull is using the wind to stay aloft without flapping its wings.

Cormorants and shags

- **There are about 40 species** of cormorant and shag, ranging in size from the pygmy cormorant at 45 cm to the flightless cormorant, which reaches about one metre in length.

- **These birds live in coastal areas** rather than the open ocean and occur all over the world, except on islands in the middle of the Pacific Ocean.

- **Cormorants and shags** have a long, thin, hooked bill for catching fish and even water snakes.

- **To catch prey**, these birds dive underwater and use their webbed feet to propel themselves along. They stay underwater for more than a minute, reaching depths of up to 30 m.

- **Strong fliers**, cormorants and shags usually move low over the water with rapid wingbeats and necks outstretched.

- **In the breeding season**, some cormorants and shags develop brightly coloured patches of skin on their faces to help them attract a mate.

▶ After fishing, cormorants hold out their wings to dry. Their feathers are not as well waterproofed as those of other birds, and this helps them to swim underwater.

- **These birds nest in colonies** on trees, cliffs or rocky islands, where they are safe from predators.

- **The flightless cormorant** lives only on some of the Galápagos Islands in the Pacific Ocean. It has very small wings and is unable to fly. In order to feed, it dives into the sea from rocks along the shore.

Pelicans

- **Pelicans are easily identified** by their long bill and massive throat pouch. They are the largest diving birds.

- **Adult pelicans** grow up to 1.8 m in length and weigh 4–7 kg. Males are larger than females. Their wingspan can measure up to 3 m.

- **There are seven species** of pelican. Most can live near bodies of freshwater, as well as oceans.

- **Most pelicans are white**, but Brown and Peruvian pelicans are dark in colour, and American white pelicans have black wing tips.

- **In some species**, the colour of the bill and pouch changes during the mating season.

- **Nearly 40,000 pelicans** come together on isolated shores or islands to breed.

- **The female pelican** builds a nest by digging a hole in the ground. She lines the hole with grass and feathers. Three days later, she lays her eggs in her new nest.

- **While fishing**, pelicans use their pouch to catch prey. Once the prey is caught, the pelican draws the pouch close to its chest to empty the water out and swallows the prey.

- **Brown and Peruvian** pelicans dive headlong into the water to catch fish.

- **Most other pelicans** swim and then pounce on their prey. Some fish in groups and drive the fish towards shallow waters where it is easier to capture them. Pelicans feed on small fish and crustaceans.

▶ The Peruvian pelican can reach a weight of 7 kg and is 1.5 m in length. It lives along the west coast of South America.

Gannets and boobies

● **The nine species** of gannets and boobies live in temperate, sub-tropical and tropical oceans all over the world. They do not live in the Southern Ocean around Antarctica.

● **These seabirds** have a narrow, streamlined body, long wings and a pointed tail. Their feet are webbed for swimming and their feathers are waterproof.

● **The largest species** is the northern gannet, which is up to one metre in length. The smallest is the Abbot's booby at 71 cm long.

● **These birds have** a strong and pointed bill with serrated edges for gripping fish.

● **To catch fish**, these birds plunge-dive into the sea from heights of about 30 m. They are travelling at about 100 km/h when they hit the water, which means they can catch food at greater depths.

● **Gannets and boobies** do not have external nostrils. Instead the nostrils are in the roof of the mouth, as in cormorants.

▶ *To cushion the impact of a dive, gannets have air sacs under the skin of the face and chest.*

● **The eyes are at the base** of the skull so the birds can scan the surface before plunging into the water. They can stay underwater for 5–30 minutes, reaching depths of 30 m and eating prey while still submerged.

● **Most gannets and boobies** lay one egg each year Chicks are fed on food regurgitated (coughed up) by the parents.

● **Blue-footed boobies** lift and spread their bright blue feet in a courtship dance to impress their partners. The name 'booby' comes from the Spanish word for clown.

Waders

● **There are over 200 species** of waders or shorebirds living in shorelines or waterways around the world.

● **Waders are usually small** or medium-sized birds with long legs and long, sensitive bills. They use their bills to probe in the mud or sand for worms, shellfish or other small animals to eat.

● **Different species** have different lengths and shapes of bill, enabling them to feed at different depths and allowing a variety of species to feed in one area.

DID YOU KNOW?

The smallest wader is the least sandpiper, at 13 cm long. The largest is the far eastern curlew, at 63 cm long.

● **Most waders are strong fliers**, often migrating long distances over water. The golden plover migrates nearly 4000 km over the Atlantic Ocean, from the coast of Canada to Brazil, where it spends the winter.

● **Nearly all waders** nest on the ground, often with little or no nesting material.

● **The eggs of waders** are often camouflaged with spots or patterns because they are not hidden in a nest.

● **Some oystercatchers** use their bills to hammer open mussels and cockles and pull out the flesh inside. Others have pointed bills to pull worms from the sand.

● **The red-necked phalarope** is an unusual bird – the male sits on the eggs and takes care of the chicks. For most birds, the female does this. In the winter, red-necked phalaropes migrate to tropical oceans.

◀ *Avocets sweep their upturned bills from side to side in shallow water, grabbing worms or small water creatures that they find. They often nest on islands, where their young are safer from attack by predators.*

Nesting seabirds

- **Nearly 95 percent** of the world's seabirds nest in large colonies for protection. The birds can warn each other of danger and help to drive attackers away from the nests and eggs.

- **Even though steep cliffs** are dangerous places for nests, it is harder for predators to reach the eggs and young. Different species nest at different levels on the same cliff, sharing out the nesting space.

▼ *Guillemots breed in tightly packed colonies on rocky islands or steep cliff faces.*

DID YOU KNOW?
Baby guillemots often fall off nesting ledges at night, plunging into the sea before their flight feathers have grown.

- **At the bottom of a cliff** nest cormorants and shags. Guillemots, razorbills and kittiwakes nest in the middle, and gannets, gulls and puffins nest near the top.

- **Murres and guillemots** lay their eggs on rocky cliff ledges. The eggs are sharply pointed at one end so they spin round instead of rolling off the cliff and into the sea.

- **Razorbill chicks** leave their nesting ledges when they are only two weeks old, but their parents feed them out at sea until they are old enough to feed themselves.

- **Kittiwakes are unusual** cliff-nesters because they build cup-shaped nests for their eggs, gluing them to cliff ledges with sticky mud and droppings.

- **Large colonies of little terns** nest on sandy beaches in summer. Members of the colony help each other by dive-bombing predators from above.

- **Puffins use their powerful bills** to dig nesting burrows on grassy cliff-tops.

Penguins

- **Penguins are big seabirds** that cannot fly. There are about 17 species, most of which live in the Antarctic.

- **Some kinds are found** as far north as the Galápagos Islands, while smaller species are found in warmer waters.

- **Larger penguins are better** at retaining heat, so they can live closer to the South Pole.

- **The emperor penguin** is the tallest at 1.2 m. The smallest is the fairy penguin (or little blue penguin), at less than 40 cm tall.

- **Penguins have a thick layer** of fat that protects them from the freezing temperatures of the region. Their feathers are waterproof.

- **These flightless birds** have black heads and wings, and a white underside. They also have sharp bills and short tails.

- **The wings of penguins** act like flippers, which help the birds to swim. Penguins are good divers and can move in water at great speeds.

- **On land**, penguins move clumsily. They are often seen sliding down slopes on their bellies.

▲ *Emperor penguin chicks huddle together in groups, called crèches, from when they are about 50 days old. Parents recognize their own chicks from the high-pitched calls that they make.*

- **Adélie penguins waddle** over 100 km every year to reach their breeding grounds. They depend on the Sun to navigate across the ice, so once the Sun sets they are at risk of losing their way.

- **Rockhopper penguins** have a tuft of yellow feathers on their head. They are named because they often jump from rock to rock.

- **Penguins have been hunted** extensively by humans for their fat and skin. Their natural enemies are sharks, whales and leopard seals.

Profile: King penguin
Super swimmer

Zooming effortlessly through the water like black-and-white torpedoes, king penguins are super swimmers. They spend up to three-quarters of their lives out at sea, only coming to land to lay their eggs and raise their chicks.

On land, they waddle along slowly, but in the water, they use their flippers to propel themselves along at speeds of about 8 km/h. King penguins can dive underwater for up to 15 minutes at a time, reaching depths of up to 500 m as they hunt for fish and squid. Deep dives tend to happen during the day, with shallow dives taking place at night. They may swim hundreds of kilometres to find food.

Before they breed, adults moult their old feathers and grow new ones. This takes up to a month and during this time, they cannot hunt for food and are forced to survive on their reserves of body fat until their new feathers have grown.

King penguins are the second largest species of penguin. Male and female king penguins look the same, although males are usually larger.

These flightless birds breed on islands in the sub-Antarctic and at the northern fringes of Antarctica.

SCIENTIFIC STUDIES

Scientists study king penguins to find out the best ways of protecting them in the future. These birds were once killed for their skins, flesh and the oil in their blubber. Today they are affected by oil spills, climate change and tourism. However, there are currently about two million breeding pairs and numbers seem to be increasing.

▶ FEATHERS
To keep warm, king penguins have four layers of feathers. The outer layer is waterproof and made of small, stiff feathers packed tightly together. Under this are three layers of fluffy feathers that trap body heat.

◀ COLOURS
Most penguins have dark backs and white fronts to camouflage them from above and below when they are in the water. The king penguin's orange ear patch is used for display, courtship and species recognition.

▶ SPINY TONGUE
The spiny tongue helps to grip food. The bill opens wider than that of any other penguin, allowing king penguins to eat bigger prey.

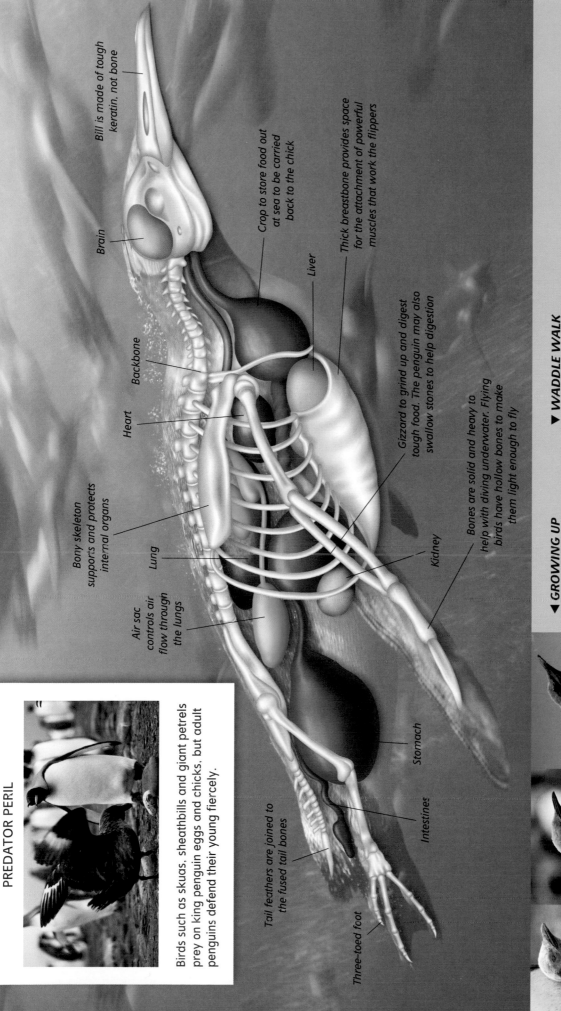

Bill is made of tough keratin, not bone

Brain

Crop to store food out at sea to be carried back to the chick

Thick breastbone provides space for the attachment of powerful muscles that work the flippers

Liver

Backbone

Heart

Gizzard to grind up and digest tough food. The penguin may also swallow stones to help digestion

Bony skeleton supports and protects internal organs

Lung

Air sac controls air flow through the lungs

Bones are solid and heavy to help with diving underwater. Flying birds have hollow bones to make them light enough to fly

Kidney

Stomach

Tail feathers are joined to the fused tail bones

Intestines

Three-toed foot

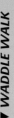

PREDATOR PERIL

Birds such as skuas, sheathbills and giant petrels prey on king penguin eggs and chicks, but adult penguins defend their young fiercely.

▶ WADDLE WALK

On land, penguins waddle upright, using sharp claws to grip rocks and ice. The stubby tail props the body upright when the penguin stands still. Penguins also toboggan on their fronts, which helps them to move faster.

◀ GROWING UP

A king penguin chick hatches after eight weeks. For the first three weeks, the chick cannot keep itself warm, so needs constant care. When it has grown a thick coat of down feathers, it huddles with other chicks in a large group (crèche) and waits to be fed by its parents. The fluffy feathers fall out as adult feathers grow.

Seals

- **Seals are marine mammals** that belong to the pinnipeds group along with walruses and sea lions.

- **There are two families** of seals: true seals and eared seals. True seals do not have external ear flaps.

- **There are 19 species** of true seals. Eared seals consist of sea lions and fur seals.

- **The limbs of seals** are modified into powerful flippers. Their torpedo-shaped bodies and ability to store oxygen make them superb swimmers.

- **True seals** use their back flippers for swimming, while eared seals use their strong front flippers to row themselves through the water. Eared seals can bring their back flippers forward, allowing them to walk on all fours on land.

- **Seals spend** most of their lives in water, coming ashore to breed and nurse their young. Some live at sea for months at a time, while others return to the shore every day.

- **Most species live in cold regions**, so they have a thick layer of fatty blubber under the skin to provide warmth and energy.

▲ Baby harp seals are born on the ice and have snowy-white coats, which act as camouflage. Mothers identify their pups by their scent.

- **Southern elephant seals** can dive to depths of up to 1500 m and can stay underwater for up to two hours. The huge males have fierce fights in the breeding season to win a group of females for mating.

- **The diet of seals** consists mainly of fish, squid, crabs and shellfish. Leopard seals are among the most aggressive hunters.

- **Killer whales**, sharks and polar bears are the natural predators of seals. Many seals are threatened by pollution, hunting and competition with the fishing industry for food resources.

Sea otters

- **The smallest ocean mammal**, the sea otter grows up to 1.4 m long. It lives in shallow coastal waters of the north Pacific Ocean, from California to Alaska.

- **This mammal** has a long, flat, rudder-like tail and large, webbed back feet, which act as flippers.

- **Sea otters spend** most of their time in the water, often floating on their backs at the surface. They even sleep like this, anchoring themselves to giant seaweeds called kelp to prevent themselves from drifting away on currents.

- **The fur of sea otters** is fine and dense, and consists of about 100,000 hairs per square centimetre to keep the animal warm.

- **Hunted for their fur** until almost extinct, sea otters are now protected and numbers have increased to about 100,000–150,000. They are still threatened by pollution and coastal development.

- **These mammals** constantly groom their fur with their teeth and paws to keep it clean and waterproof.

- **Sea otters** dive to depths of up to 75 m to gather food such as mussels, snails, crabs and urchins.

- **Social animals**, sea otters live in groups of between ten and 100 or more, called rafts.

- **Sea otters** give birth in the water. Females usually have one pup and carry it on their chest.

- **Pups stay at the surface** while their mother dives for food, but learn to follow her and find food for themselves.

▼ Sea otters are one of the few mammals to use tools. They float on their back, place a rock on their chest and smash shellfish against the rock to break them open so they can eat the flesh.

Whales and dolphins

▼ *Dusky dolphins are very agile and acrobatic.*

● **Whales spend all their lives** in the oceans. They belong to a group of mammals called cetaceans, which includes the small whales we call dolphins and porpoises.

● **Cetaceans range in size** from the vaquita, or gulf porpoise, which is less than 1.5 m long, to the blue whale, which can reach a length of over 30 m.

● **Whales hold their** breath underwater. They come up to the surface to breathe air through nostrils called blowholes on the top of the head. The blowholes stay closed underwater.

● **The spout** (blow) that can be seen rising from the blowhole is stale air that condenses and vaporizes the moment it is released into the atmosphere.

● **Whales are divided** into two main groups: toothed whales and baleen whales. Together, these groups contain about 80 known species.

● **Toothed whales** have small teeth, which they use to kill prey such as squid. This group includes dolphins, killer whales, sperm whales, beluga whales and porpoises.

● **Toothed whales emit sound waves** that are bounced off an object, revealing its size, shape and location. This is known as echolocation.

● **Echolocation** is used to distinguish between prey and non-prey objects.

● **Baleen whales** are toothless. They trap prey in sieve-like structures hanging from their upper jaws. Bowhead whales have the longest baleen, which reaches a length of about 4 m.

● **The blue whale** has a call that is louder than a jet plane. It reaches a level of 188 decibels, whereas a jet plane only reaches 140 decibels. A blue whale's call travels long distances through the oceans, perhaps for hundreds of kilometres.

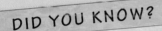

DID YOU KNOW?

The heart of a blue whale is the size of a small car, but its eye is only as big as a teacup.

▶ *A female grey whale and newborn calf. If threatened, a mother will defend her calf fiercely from predators.*

Baleen whales

- **The baleen whales** include the largest whales, such as the blue, humpback, grey, fin, sei, minke, bowhead and right whales.

- **The largest family of baleen whales** is the Balaenopteridae, also known as the rorqual family. These whales have 25–100 throat grooves, which look like pleats and allow the throat to expand as the whales feed.

- **Baleen is a strong**, flexible material made of keratin, the material that your fingernails and hair are made of. When a whale is born, the baleen is soft and short, but it grows and thickens. Baleen grows throughout a whale's life and the ends wear down all the time.

- **The outer edge** of a baleen plate is smooth, but the inner edge is frayed to form a fringe. This overlaps to sieve fish, crustaceans and plankton from the water.

- **Some baleen whales** feed by gulping large amounts of water and then using their tongue to force the water out between their baleen plates.

- **Other baleen whales** swim along with their mouths wide open, skimming and filtering food as they go.

- **Baleen whales** have two blowholes. When the whales surface, they expel stale air through these blowholes, which makes a V-shaped pattern in the air.

▲ Baleen whales, such as this bowhead whale, have hundreds of baleen plates in their jaws – bowhead whales have about 350 pairs of plates.

Blue whale

- **Blue whales** are the largest creatures ever to have lived on Earth.

- **Their average length** is 25 m but some can grow to more than 30 m.

- **These whales** are blue-grey in colour with light patches on their backs.

▼ An adult blue whale weighs about 160 tonnes – that's the combined weight of 30 big bull elephants.

- **The diet of a blue whale** consists of small fish, plankton and krill in enormous quantities. They can eat over 4 tonnes of krill every day.

- **Blue whales** have been known to gather in groups of 60 or more. However, they are largely solitary animals.

- **The body is streamlined** with a large tail fin. The dorsal fin is small, while the tail is thick and large. Blue whales have splashguards in front of their blowholes.

- **Blue whales** are migratory animals. They live near the tropics during winter and migrate towards icy waters in summer.

- **Blue whales** are relatively slow swimmers. However, if threatened, these animals can swim at a speed of up to 50 km/h.

- **Merciless hunting** over several decades has caused the blue whale population to decline drastically. It is currently an endangered species, and between 10,000 and 25,000 are thought to exist worldwide.

Humpback whale

- **Humpbacks** are large baleen whales. They are one of the most active whales and often leap out of the water.

- **Found in most parts of the world**, humpbacks migrate to icy waters in the north and south during summer. In winter, they breed in tropical waters.

- **Humpbacks have a flat head** that has fleshy bumps (tubercles). The body is dark, with white patches. The underside is off-white in colour.

- **The humpback grows** up to 15 m in length. It is named after a hump on which the whale's dorsal fin is located.

- **The tail fin** measures nearly 5.5 m across and has black-and-white patterns. These patterns are unique to each whale, so scientists use them to identify and monitor humpbacks.

- **Humpbacks feed on** shrimps, krill and small fish. They have various methods of feeding.

▲ *Humpback whales scoop up food from the water with their huge mouths.*

- **When lunge-feeding**, the humpback opens its mouth wide and swims through a group of prey.

- **When tail-flicking**, the whale lies with its belly below the surface using its tail to flick prey into its mouth.

- **Bubble-netting** is a spectacular feeding habit. The humpbacks submerge and swim in circles as they blow out air around a school of fish. This creates a wall of bubbles, forcing the fish to move to the surface, which makes them easy prey.

- **Male humpbacks** are known for their songs. The sounds vary from squeaks to wails. They are usually heard in the breeding season.

DID YOU KNOW?

Humpbacks travel over 8000 km on their migration from Antarctica to Central America each year.

Fin whale

- **After the blue whale**, the fin whale is the second-largest animal in the world.

- **It can reach a** huge 27 m in length.

- **Fin whales eat krill**, but also include small fish in their diet. They trap food between their baleen plates.

- **Fin whales** have an unusual lower jaw, which is white on the right side and grey-black on the left side. The colour of the baleen plates is the same as that of the jaw.

- **Groups of 100** or more fin whales may gather at feeding grounds. They have 50–200 pleats on their lower jaw, which expand to gulp in water and prey.

- **Males make** long, low sounds during the breeding season. This calls are extremely loud, reaching 184–186 decibels.

- **Calves are born** after a gestation of 11–12 months. They double in size during the last two months of development inside their mother.

▲ *Fin whales are the fastest whales, with swimming speeds of up to 56 km/h when hunting small fish.*

- **Fin whale calves** are about 6 m long when born and weigh about 2 tonnes.

- **Commercial whaling** in the 20th century killed off about 70 percent of the world's fin whales. There are no reliable estimates of global numbers at the moment but these magnificent whales are an endangered species.

DID YOU KNOW?

When a fin whale comes to the water's surface and breathes out, its spout can reach heights of 10–15 m.

Minke whale

- **The second-smallest** of the baleen whales (after the pygmy right whale), the minke (pronounced 'minkey') whale grows to between 8 and 10 m long.

- **They are the most common** of the baleen whales, with a population of some 665,000. Minke whales escaped much of the 20th century whaling due to their smaller size.

- **Minke whales** feed mainly on krill in the Southern Hemisphere and fish such as capelin, cod and herring in the Northern Hemisphere. They are usually solitary but may gather in groups at feeding areas.

- **Food is filtered** from the water with baleen plates hanging down from either side of the whale's top jaws.

- **Minke whales** are a type of rorqual whale, with 50–70 pleats or grooves in the throat. This allows the throat to expand widely when feeding, enabling them to take in large quantities of water and food.

- **Males make sounds** as loud as 152 decibels, which is louder than a jet taking off. Sound travels well through the ocean waters, allowing the whales to communicate with others of their kind.

- **Calves are born** after a gestation period of about ten months and are about 3 m long at birth. They drink their mother's milk for about five months.

- **Minke whales** are found in all oceans but often prefer icy waters and the open sea.

- **In the Northern Hemisphere**, minke whales have a white band on each flipper. Those living in Antarctic waters have grey flippers, and are probably a different species.

▶ *A slender whale with a pointed snout, the minke whale can reach speeds of 30 km/h and dive for up to 20 minutes.*

Right whale

- **The three species** of large baleen whales called right whales are among the most endangered.

- **Right whales live** in the North Atlantic, the eastern North Pacific and the Southern Ocean.

- **The name 'right'** was given to these great whales by early whalers because they were the 'right' whales to hunt. They were easy to catch as they were slow swimmers, lived close to shore, floated when killed and contained a lot of valuable oil in their blubber.

- **These huge whales** can reach 18 m in length and weigh up to 100 tonnes.

- **Right whales have** rough patches of skin on the head, called callosities. These are often colonized by whale lice. Individual whales can be recognized from the pattern of their callosities.

- **Right whales filter plankton**, krill and crustaceans from the ocean with 200–300 baleen plates, which reach up to 10 m in length.

- **Calves are born** after a gestation period of about a year and measure 4–5 m in length. They stay with their mothers for a year before becoming independent.

- **The northern right whale** and the North Pacific right whale are probably the most endangered of the great whales, with only a few hundred individuals remaining. Even the southern right whale has only 3200 mature females in its population.

◀ *Right whales are almost black and have massive, rounded bodies. Their flippers are wide and the tail may reach 7 m across.*

DID YOU KNOW?

Unlike other baleen whales, the right whale does not have a grooved throat.

Toothed whales

● **There are over 70 species** of toothed whale, which make up almost 90 percent of the cetacean group.

● **Toothed whales** are generally smaller than baleen whales and include dolphins, porpoises, pilot whales, beluga whales, narwhals, beaked whales, killer whales and sperm whales.

● **The largest toothed whale** is the sperm whale, which reaches lengths of 18 m.

● **Toothed whales** have one blowhole in the top of the head, whereas baleen whales have two.

▼ *Male narwhals fight with their tusks in the breeding season.*

● **Active hunters**, toothed whales have peg-like teeth to grip prey such as fish, squid and, in some cases, seals or other whales.

● **Toothed whales** have a larger throat than baleen whales and swallow food whole or in large pieces.

● **Most species** of toothed whale have a waxy organ, called a melon in the forehead. This helps to focus the clicking sounds the whales make for echolocation.

● **Echolocation is a method** of locating prey by sending out sounds and listening for the echoes that bounce back.

● **Narwhals have only two teeth** in the top jaw. In most males, and some females, one of these teeth develops into a 2–3-m-long, spiral tusk, growing out through a hole in the top lip.

● **One large family** of toothed whales (over 20 species) is the beaked whales. Beaked whales are almost toothless, although males have one pair of teeth, which they may use to fight for females.

Sperm whale

● **The sperm whale** is the world's largest toothed animal. Males are 16–18 m long, while females reach lengths of 12–14 m. Males weigh about 50 tonnes, about twice as much as females.

● **Males reach full size** at 50 years old and live for up to 80 years.

● **The sperm whale** has a very large head, which takes up about one-third of its length.

● **The spout** of a sperm whale reaches up to 15 m above the surface and is angled to the left.

● **Sperm whales** were once hunted for the oil that was obtained from their blubber and a part of their head called the spermaceti organ. Scientists are not sure what this organ does. It may help the whale to make deep dives or focus the sounds made during echolocation.

● **By slowing their heart rate** and directing blood to the brain and other essential organs, sperm whales may stay underwater for up to two hours.

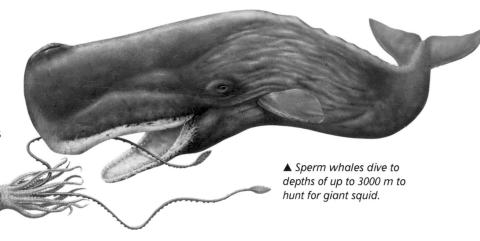

▲ *Sperm whales dive to depths of up to 3000 m to hunt for giant squid.*

● **In the gut** of sperm whales, a substance called ambergris forms around the beaks of the squid they have eaten. This was once used to make perfume and was one reason so many sperm whales were killed between the 17th and 20th centuries. They are still endangered today.

● **Sperm whales** have 20–26 pairs of cone-shaped teeth in the bottom jaw but do not seem to use their teeth for feeding. Males may use their teeth to fight rivals.

● **Calves are born** after a gestation period of at least a year. They are 4 m long at birth and weigh one tonne.

Profile: Killer whale

Pod predator

Active and highly intelligent, these whales are called 'killer' because they are top ocean predators. Killer whales are the largest-ever hunters of mammals, even attacking enormous prey, such as blue whales. They are not known to attack humans.

Killer whales live and hunt in groups called pods, which are made up of four to 40 closely related individuals, led by the oldest female. They communicate using clicks and whistles and each pod may have its own 'language'.

Fish, squid, seals, sea lions, walruses, seabirds, turtles, otters, porpoises, other whales and even polar bears and moose are eaten by killer whales. Diet depends on the region the whales live in and the type of pod they belong to. Resident pods stay in one place. They tend to eat fish and rarely hunt mammals.

Transient (travelling) pods specialize in hunting marine mammals but sometimes eat fish. Pod members work together to encircle prey before attacking. Young whales (calves) learn how to hunt by watching adults, which also protect the calves from possible predators. A baby killer whale develops for about 17 months inside its mother before it is born. It drinks its mother's milk for a year or more.

WHALE THREATS

Tourists watching killer whales from boats may disturb the whales and disrupt their feeding. Other threats include pollution, being shot by fishermen and reductions in fish populations as a result of climate change.

▲ TEETH
The large, cone-shaped teeth of killer whales are good for ripping and tearing, but not for chewing. The whales swallow food in chunks and their throats are big enough to accommodate small seals and walruses whole.

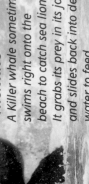

◄ HUNTING
A Killer whale sometimes swims right onto the beach to catch sea lions. It grabs its prey in its jaws and slides back into deep water to feed.

Melon focuses any sounds the whale makes into a beam, which travels through the water. Echoes of the sounds help the whale to detect objects such as prey

Powerful jaws and strong teeth

Barrel-shaped rib cage protects the heart and lungs

Lung

Heart rate can be slowed when diving to conserve oxygen

Finger and thumb bones in flipper, with thick pads of cartilage between them

Liver

50–54 vertebrae but no bones in the tail flukes

Intestines

Stomach

Small hip bone (pelvis) but no back leg bone

Kidney

Lower jawbone is filled with fat and conducts sounds to bones in the ears

▼ PODS

Killer whales are sometimes called 'wolves of the sea' because they hunt in groups, rather like a wolf pack does on land. Pods may join up to form larger groups, which can consist of up to 500 individuals.

▲ SPY-HOPPING

To take a good look around, killer whales let their bodies hang vertically in the water and lift their heads above the surface. This behaviour is known as spy-hopping and is often done to look for prey.

Killer whale

- **Despite their name**, killer whales, also known as orcas, are the largest members of the dolphin family.

- **They have** a black body with white patches on their underside and behind each eye.

- **Found in oceans** across the world, killer whales prefer to live in colder waters. They do not migrate in summer like great whales, and often live close to the coast.

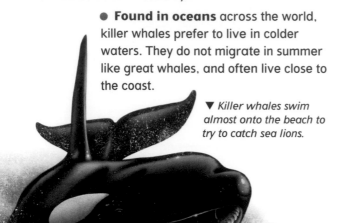

▼ *Killer whales swim almost onto the beach to try to catch sea lions.*

- **Killer whales** reach lengths of 8–10 m. They have sharp, hooked teeth, which are used to rip prey apart.

- **The diet** of killer whales is varied. They largely prey on fish, squid, sharks and warm-blooded animals such as seals, seabirds and larger whales.

- **Also known as** the 'wolves of the sea', killer whales hunt in groups (pods) and can tackle prey of any size.

- **Killer whale pods** are divided into resident and transient pods. Resident pods consist of between 5–50 members that communicate with whistles and high-pitched screams.

- **Transient pods** have a maximum of seven members that feed mainly on marine mammals. They do not communicate frequently with each other.

Dolphins

- **Dolphins are small toothed whales** and there are about 32 species. They have a beak-shaped snout and are very active and playful mammals.

- **Found in all oceans**, dolphins are powerful swimmers. They are often spotted riding on waves, probably to conserve energy.

- **Dolphins may take** deep dives, but usually swim just a few metres beneath the surface of the water. They usually stay underwater for just a few minutes but can remain submerged for up to half an hour.

▼ *Some dolphins swim at up to 40 km/h, which is more than three times faster than the fastest human swimmers.*

- **Like all toothed whales**, dolphins have only one blowhole in the top of the head for breathing air.

- **Dolphins use echolocation** to hunt and navigate through cloudy waters. They emit a series of high-pitched sound pulses, which bounce off prey or obstacles, enabling dolphins to locate them.

- **These animals hunt in groups** by chasing their prey. They then surround it and catch it with their powerful jaws.

- **A dolphin's brain**, in relation to the size of its body, is larger than the brains of humans, chimpanzees and other great apes. Dolphins are very intelligent mammals and may even have a language of their own.

- **A baby dolphin** is born tail first. The mother is often helped by another female dolphin during the birth. The calf stays with its mother for two to three years.

- **Wild dolphins can live** to be 50 years old, although their average lifespan is 17 years. Members of dolphin groups (called pods) form strong bonds with each other and may even support sick or dying pod members.

DID YOU KNOW?

Dolphins have two stomachs – one for digesting food and one for storing food.

Porpoises

● **Porpoises are small**, toothed whales. They are close relatives of dolphins.

● **Usually smaller than dolphins**, porpoises rarely grow to more than 2.2 m. They are grey, blue or black in colour.

● **Unlike most dolphins**, porpoises do not have a pointed snout. A porpoise's head is blunt and rounded.

● **Porpoises have a triangular fin** mid-way down the back, whereas dolphins have a curved fin.

● **Another difference** between porpoises and dolphins is their teeth. Porpoises have spade- or shovel-shaped teeth, whereas dolphins have teeth shaped like cones.

● **The Asian finless porpoise** has a ridge of small, rounded bumps just behind the area where other porpoises have a triangular fin on the back.

● **Dall's porpoise** is known for the splash it makes with its tail. This is called a 'rooster-tail', and has earned this species its other name of 'spray porpoise'.

● **The harbour**, or common, porpoise has the shortest lifespan of all cetaceans – up to 20 or 25 years. Most only survive about ten years in the wild.

● **Spectacled porpoises** have black patches around their eyes, which are surrounded by a white line. These resemble spectacles.

▼ *The spectacled porpoise has distinctive colouration. It lives in the Southern Ocean, around the lower tip of South America and near islands such as the Falklands and South Georgia.*

Beluga

● **Beluga whales** have a playful nature and this, along with their unusual colour, makes them popular attractions in aquariums. They are related to dolphins.

● **As they have narrow necks**, belugas can nod and shake their heads from side to side.

● **The beluga's scientific name**, *Delphinapterus leucas*, means 'white dolphin without wings', referring to the absence of a dorsal fin.

● **The beluga's diet** consists of crabs, squid, shrimps and fish. They use their teeth to grab prey rather than to chew it.

● **Highly social animals**, belugas tend to travel in groups of 5–20 members, usually led by a single male. During migrations, groups can exceed 10,000 members.

● **These whales emit** various sounds, from whistles to chirps and squeaks. They are the most vocal whales, earning them the nickname of sea canaries.

● **Belugas are hunted** by killer whales. The young are often killed by polar bears. It is not uncommon to find adult belugas bearing scars from polar bear attacks.

DID YOU KNOW?
Belugas do not have a dorsal fin, which makes swimming under ice much easier.

▼ *The milky-white colour of the beluga matches its habitat, in the icy Arctic Ocean. Young belugas are born grey, turning white as they get older.*

Sea lions

● **Sea lions are eared seals** – unlike true seals, they have external ear flaps and their flippers are quite big.

● **These extremely vocal animals** make a roaring noise, which gives them their name. They are brownish in colour, with males being darker than females.

● **Sea lions use their flippers** to swim and paddle in water as well as to walk on land.

● **Being highly social creatures**, sea lions swim in large groups.

● **Steller's sea lion** is the largest sea lion – males can grow up to 3 m in length. They are found in the northern waters of the Pacific Ocean.

● **Adult male** Steller's sea lions have a thick neck covered by long, coarse hair.

● **The diet of a sea lion** includes mainly fish, crabs, squid, octopus and clams. Steller's sea lion also feeds on seals and small otters.

● **Unlike other sea lions**, California sea lions do not have lion-like manes. They can swim at top speeds of 40 km/h and stay underwater for nearly ten minutes before surfacing to breathe.

● **Killer whales** are the biggest enemies of sea lions. Sharks are also known to hunt California sea lions.

● **A large number of sea lions** die as a result of getting caught in fishing nets, and there are now laws restricting the hunting of them. Steller's sea lion has been declared endangered.

▲ *Australian sea lions are very social animals, gathering in large groups, especially in the breeding season. There are just 3000–5000 animals surviving, and they breed only on mainland Australia and nearby islands.*

Sea cows

● **There are four species** of sea cows alive today, one species of dugong and three species of manatee.

● **Sea cows** are also called sirenians, after the sirens (mermaids) of Greek mythology. It is thought that sailors mistook sea cows for creatures that were half-human and half-fish, giving rise to the mermaid legends.

● **Dugongs are found** in the tropical waters of the Indian and Pacific oceans. Manatees are found off the Caribbean islands, the southeast coast of the United States and West Africa.

● **Steller's sea cow**, one of the largest species, is now extinct. It was hunted for its meat and skin.

● **Sea cows breathe** through two nostrils at the end of their muzzle. They can close off the nostrils with a flap of skin when they are underwater.

● **Manatees have** long, rounded bodies and their average length is 3.5 m. They are mostly grey in colour.

● **Manatees and dugongs** are slow swimmers.

▶ *Sea cows feed on sea grasses, using lip pads to grip plants and rows of stiff bristles under the lips to guide food to the mouth.*

● **Dugongs are quite strong swimmers**, with a forked tail similar to that of a dolphin. Manatees have a paddle-shaped tail and can roll and spiral in the water by curling and twisting the edges of their tail.

Fishing

● **People use a variety** of fishing methods – from hand, spear or bow fishing to netting, fishing hooks and lines, trapping or dredging, even explosions.

● **Fishing nets** are made by knotting a fine thread to form a mesh, which traps the fish. In gill nets, fish are caught when their gill covers catch in the mesh.

● **Trawlers tow** heavy conical nets (trawls) through the seawater or along the seabed. The mouth of the net stays open while it is being towed, scooping up shoals of fish, which are then lifted with winches onto the trawler.

● **Longline fishing** uses long strings of baited hooks, which may be up to 20 km long with up to 12,000 hooks.

● **Purse seining** is a way of catching fish in mid-water or near the surface in a deep curtain of netting that is supported at the surface by floats. Unlike trawl nets, the mouths of seiner nets are drawn together (like closing a purse) before they are hauled on board. A large purse seine net can be one kilometre long and 200 m deep.

● **Creels and pots** are small baited traps that attract prey such as crabs and lobsters. They are set down on the seabed, often in long strings, with floating buoys attached to show where they are.

● **Dredges are used** to collect scallops or oysters from the seabed but the process destroys sea creatures. They may also be farmed or collected by divers.

● **At least 43 percent** of fish supplies around the world come from fish farms, which cause problems such as pollution of the surrounding waters and the spread of disease to wild fish.

◀ Fishermen aboard the Breton trawler Amaryllis haul in their catch from the Greenland Sea, off the coast of Iceland.

Ships and boats

● **Modern ships** include commercial ships, such as cargo and passenger ships, as well as military ships, such as aircraft carriers. Smaller vessels include rowing boats, motorboats, jet boats and yachts.

● **Cargo ships** transport goods such as cars, gas and metals. There are two main kinds – container ships that carry their cargo in huge containers, and bulk carriers.

● **Bulk carriers** are single-deck vessels that carry unpackaged dry cargo such as grain. They have one large container and cargo is poured into it through openings in its roof.

● **Tankers are the most widely used** cargo ships. They transport crude oil, petroleum or chemicals.

● **Supertankers** are the biggest ships. Too big to approach ports, they offload cargo into smaller vessels.

● **Roll-on-roll-off** (RORO) vessels and lighter aboard ships (LASH) are alternatives to container ships. RORO ships have openings on their sides and stern through which cars and trucks can be driven aboard.

● **The LASH vessel** is a cargo ship with a crane. Cargo is placed in barges that are loaded onto a mothership.

▲ Massive cruise ships cater for the needs of growing numbers of tourists worldwide.

● **Tugs are small** but extremely powerful motorized ships. They are used to guide ships into docks and to tow defective ships, barges and equipment across open seas.

● **Icebreakers** are tough, specialized vessels that clear ice in rivers and seas in order to create a passage.

● **Aircraft carriers** are massive warships that carry military aircraft. They have flight decks to support the take-off and landing of fighters and bombers.

Submersibles

- **A submersible** is an underwater research vessel. It is primarily used to conduct scientific research and for military and industrial purposes.

- **Submersibles help with the studies** of undersea geological activity, marine life and mineral deposits. They also help to check on oil rigs. Those involved in research often accompany a research vessel.

- **Navies use submersibles** for a variety of tasks, such as submarine rescue and repair, and mine detection.

- **Wreck divers** use submersibles for salvage operations, such as recovering planes or equipment that have sunk to the ocean depths.

- **Pressurized submersibles** are designed to operate in very deep waters, and are capable of withstanding extreme pressure.

- **An ROV** (Remotely Operated Vehicle) is a robot submersible that is tethered to a ship by a thick cable and controlled by a 'pilot' on board the ship. The biggest ROVs are lifted in and out of the water by cranes.

- **ROVs are used** for pipeline and oil rig inspections.

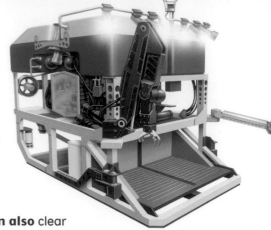

▶ Jason is an ROV that has been used to explore hydrothermal vents on the ocean floor.

- **They can also** clear mines, lay cables and recover ships or planes from the seabed.

- **ROVs are equipped with lights**, cameras, underwater microphones, thrusters (to move position) and instruments such as temperature sensors and depth sensors. Some ROVs have a robot arm for moving or cutting things or taking scientific samples.

- **Scientists use ROVs** to explore the oceans in areas where it is difficult for people to go, such as under the Antarctic ice sheets or in particularly deep water.

- **Mini and micro ROVs** can be used by one person on a small boat. A mini ROV weighs about 15 kg and a micro ROV can weigh as little as 3 kg or less.

Minerals

- **Oceans contain minerals** that form in the oceans themselves, as well as those that wash into the water from the land.

- **Seawater contains** about 3.5 percent dissolved solids, including more than 60 chemical elements, such as potassium, magnesium and manganese. Extraction of minerals depends on cost, ownership and technology.

▼ Salt is one mineral obtained from the oceans. It can be extracted by evaporating the water to leave the salt behind.

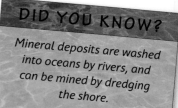

DID YOU KNOW?

Mineral deposits are washed into oceans by rivers, and can be mined by dredging the shore.

- **The International Seabed Authority**, which is part of the United Nations, controls mining in international waters. It aims to protect the ocean from the harmful effects of mining, such as pollution.

- **Magnesium is the only metal** extracted directly from seawater. It can also be obtained by mining minerals such as magnesite or dolomite from ancient ocean deposits.

- **Huge deposits of manganese nodules** have been discovered on the seabed. These nodules primarily consist of manganese and iron. Traces of copper, cobalt and nickel can also be found in them.

- **In 2009**, advances in technology made it possible to extract minerals from the deep ocean floor, about 1.6 km below the surface.

- **Deep-sea mines** are likely to cause noise, waste and pollution as well as damaging ecosystems such as hydrothermal vent communities.

Fossil fuels

- **Fossil fuels**, such as petroleum and coal, are extracted from the fossilized remains of animals and plants from millions of years ago.

- **Crude oil** is formed from tiny plants and animals that lived in the ancient oceans. Sediment settled on the mud, and heat and pressure turned it into crude oil.

- **Natural gas** is primarily formed by the decaying of dead plankton that has accumulated on the ocean floor.

- **Crude oil and natural gas** fill porous (reservoir) rocks. As reservoir rocks are normally filled with water, the fuel, which is lighter than water, travels up until it reaches non porous rocks. These trap the fuel to create a reservoir. Coal is a fossil fuel formed from decomposed plants.

- **About half the carbon dioxide** released into the atmosphere by burning fossil fuels has dissolved in the oceans. This is making the oceans more acidic, which could have a serious impact on ocean food chains.

- **Acidic oceans** make corals grow more slowly or their skeletons become less dense. The corals are worn away, threatening the ecosystem.

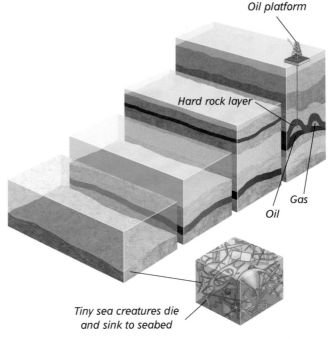

Oil platform

Hard rock layer

Gas

Oil

Tiny sea creatures die and sink to seabed

▲ *The remains of tiny sea creatures sink to the seabed and are buried under sediments. Slowly they turn into oil or gas by heat and pressure.*

- **Some scientists** have suggested storing carbon dioxide beneath the seabed. The carbon dioxide would be pumped down in liquid form and take millions of years to leak out.

Drilling for oil

- **The search for oil** in the oceans is increasing. Natural resources found in the seabed are extracted and refined to produce fuel.

- **Oil companies** usually build offshore drilling rigs to extract resources from the seabed. Rigs are platforms set up in the sea, some distance from the shore.

- **Oil rigs are** made of steel or concrete that can withstand huge waves and storms. Alaskan oil rigs also have to withstand icy waters and ice floes.

- **Rigs are equipped** with drills that tunnel several hundred metres into the ocean floor.

- **Once the presence** of crude oil is confirmed, it is extracted and sent to refineries where it is processed into petroleum and petroleum products, such as kerosene.

- **Some oil rigs** are huge platforms that drop an anchor and float on the water. These platforms have air-filled supports and are called semi-submersible rigs.

▶ *Drilling rigs are built to extract oil and gas from rocks beneath the ocean. Stormy weather at sea often makes this a dangerous and expensive activity.*

- **Permanent oil rigs** are built in areas where production is high and multiple oil wells can be drilled.

- **Sometimes pressure builds up** in the underground wells, causing blow-outs. When a blow-out occurs the drilling hole explodes, spilling oil into the water.

- **Blow-out preventers** control pressure in underwater wells while drilling.

- **One oil rig** can be linked to as many as 80 wells and reach over 1.6 km beneath the surface of the oceans.

Oil spills

● **Less than eight percent** of the oil spills in the oceans come from leaking ships, oil tankers or oil wells.

● **Most waste oil** comes from oily water washed into the oceans from farms, factories and cities (including waste oil from car engines), routine maintenance of ships and recreational boating.

● **Oil spills happen** when people are careless or do not respect the law. Wars, terrorists or natural disasters, such as hurricanes, may also cause oil spills.

● **The damage caused** depends on the amount and type of oil and the location of the spill, as well as temperature, wind and weather.

● **Oil spills harm all ocean life**, from plankton, seaweed and fish to birds, sea otters and whales. Oil may block a whale's blowhole or poison the fish or plankton it eats.

● **In 1989**, the *Exxon Valdez* oil tanker ran aground at Prince William Sound in Alaska, spilling enough oil to fill about 125 Olympic-sized swimming pools. About 2800 sea otters and 250,000 seabirds died. It took 10,000 workers four summers to clean up the spill.

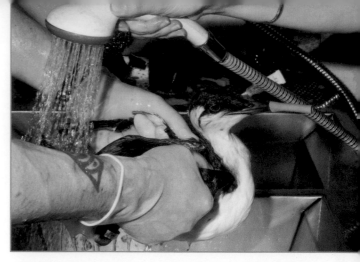

▲ *If seabirds get covered in oil, their feathers no longer keep them warm and waterproof. The birds may also eat the oil and poison themselves.*

● **Two major spills** occured in the 1990s. The *Braer* tanker spilled 26 million tonnes of oil off the Shetland Islands (Scotland, UK) in 1993 and the *Sea Empress* spilled 18 million tonnes off Wales (UK) in 1996.

● **To stop the spread** of an oil spill, booms can be placed around a tanker to absorb oil, the oil can be skimmed or burned off, or chemicals can be used to break it up. High-pressure hoses clean up beaches if oil washes ashore.

Ocean pollution

● **Excessive human activity** in coastal areas has increased pollution and caused damage to ocean life.

● **The discharge** of industrial waste and human sewage into the sea is the most common form of pollution. This affects marine life and makes the sea unfit for bathing.

● **The pollution** that enters oceans can be categorized as coming from 'point sources' and 'non-point sources'. Sewer pipes and industrial waste pipes are examples of point sources, as the discharge is from a single, identifiable point.

● **Non-point sources** of pollution are harder to tackle. They include water or sewage from farms containing fertilizers with a high chemical content.

● **Some chemicals** found in pesticides are biodegradable, and their effects are minimal. Others remain dangerous for a long time.

● **Petroleum and oil products** enter the water through spills from ships and leakages from pipelines and storage tanks.

● **Power stations** are a major source of pollution. The water they discharge is usually hot and so it alters the temperature of the water, adversely affecting marine life.

● **Many beaches** have become tourist attractions. Plastic litter left on beaches is a hazard to marine life.

● **Metals such as copper** and lead enter the oceans from dumped industrial waste and automobile emissions. These metals can lead to health problems in animals and people.

▼ *Pipes discharging untreated sewage onto beaches are a major problem for people and ocean life.*

DID YOU KNOW?

Eighty percent of ocean pollution comes from sources on land, such as cars and farms.

Ocean power

- **The energy** of movement in the ocean's waves, tides and currents can be used to produce electrical power.

- **The moving water** is used to push a turbine wheel around and this movement energy can be converted into electrical energy inside a generator.

- **A tidal power station** is built inside a dam or barrage across a narrow bay or the mouth of a river where it meets the ocean. As the tide flows in and out of the dam, it generates electricity.

▶ *Offshore wind farms could produce more energy than those based on land, but they are more costly.*

- **Underwater turbines** can be used to collect the energy in ocean and tidal currents.

- **Some wave-power devices** are fixed to the ocean floor where they are less likely to be damaged by storms and strong winds and cause less visual pollution than if they were on the surface.

- **Other wave-energy systems** include devices that use the rise and fall of the waves inside a concrete chamber, and shoreline devices that channel waves into reservoirs that concentrate wave power.

- **Groups of large windmills,** or wind turbines, called wind farms can be built in the oceans near the shore, where they generate energy from the winds moving over the waves. These wind farms may disturb the ocean currents and marine ecosystems.

Sea levels

- **Sea levels have risen** and fallen for millions of years, due to changes in climate or movement inside the Earth, causing the ocean floor to move up or down.

- **During the last Ice Age**, sea levels fell by about 90 m because so much water was frozen as ice sheets on land.

- **Melting of the ice caps** at the end of the last Ice Age caused sea levels to rise about 120 m. Valleys in Norway and Alaska that had once been filled by glaciers became flooded. These watery valleys are called fjords.

- **A rise in sea level** is partly caused by melting snow, glaciers and ice sheets when the Earth's temperature increases.

- **Sea levels also rise** because the oceans expand and take up more space as the sea warms up.

- **Some scientists estimate** that sea levels could rise by up to 1.5 m by the year 2100. Other estimates suggest a smaller rise of about 28–43 cm.

- **About 80–90 percent** of Bangladesh is within a metre of sea level and islands in the Pacific, such as the Maldives, are just a few metres above sea level.

▲ *Sea levels are thought to have risen by about 10–25 cm over the past 100 years.*

- **The Thames barrier** was built across the river Thames in London to stop the city being flooded by high tides and storm waves from the North Sea. Rising sea levels would threaten other coastal cities around the world, such as New York, Los Angeles, Lagos, Shanghai, Rio de Janeiro and Tokyo.

Coastal defences

- **There are two** ways that coasts are defended against erosion and flooding – hard engineering and soft engineering.

- **Hard engineering** includes defences such as sea walls, cages of boulders (gabions), slatted barriers (revetments) and groynes.

- **Hard engineering solutions** are designed to stop waves hitting the shore but are expensive and often cause problems further along the coast. They need regular maintenance and take away the beauty of beaches.

- **In tropical areas**, mangrove swamps protect coasts from storms and floods. The roots of mangroves also trap mud, helping to build up the coastline.

- **Soft engineering** uses natural processes to manage coasts and sometimes lets the sea erode coasts rather than trying to fight nature.

- **When beach material** is washed away, more mud or sand can be added to build up the beach and protect the land behind the beach from flooding.

- **Plants such as marram grass** can be planted on sand dunes to stop them being blown away. The grass roots bind the sand together and protect the dunes, which provide a defence against floods.

- **Planting salt marshes** on the shoreline helps to protect the beach and slow down erosion by the waves. It also creates a habitat for wildlife, such as wading birds.

◄ *Groynes are low wooden fences on beaches. They are placed at right angles to the coast and help to stop beach material from being washed along the coast by the waves.*

Global warming

- **Global warming** is a rapid rise in the average temperature of the whole planet as a result of the greenhouse effect.

- **The greenhouse effect** is the process by which certain gases in the Earth's atmosphere trap some of the heat given off by the Earth and keep the planet warm enough for life to survive. Without greenhouse gases, the Earth's average temperature would be −18°C – too cold for life.

- **Greenhouse gases** include water vapour, carbon dioxide, methane, nitrous oxide, CFCs and ozone. Water vapour is the most common of these, and is responsible for about 60 percent of the natural greenhouse effect.

- **Most scientists** think that deforestation and pollution have increased the amounts of greenhouse gases in the atmosphere, causing the planet to warm up faster than it would do naturally. In the last 150 years, the amount of carbon dioxide in the atmosphere has increased by about one third.

- **Scientists predict** that global temperatures could rise by 2–5°C by the end of the 21st century, making the world hotter than it has been for more than 100,000 years.

- **Global warming** is already causing problems, such as rising sea levels, flooding, droughts, wildfires, extreme weather and the spread of diseases such as malaria.

- **One hundred million people** live in places that are only one metre above sea level, so they are very vulnerable to even small rises in sea levels.

◄ *The Maldives could sink beneath the waves within 100 years as a result of global warming. Wave breakers have been built as a protective measure.*

Coral reef threats

- **The impact of global warming** on the oceans is most visible in the bleaching (die-off caused by stress) of coral reefs.

- **Reefs are very delicate structures**, formed by coral polyps. The main food source of polyps is the unicellular algae, called zooxanthellae, which live within their tissues.

- **The algae** feed on nitrogen waste produced by corals. They also produce food using sunlight (photosynthesis). The corals rely on this to survive.

- **As well as providing food**, the algae also give the reefs their colour, which attracts many other marine creatures.

- **Reefs lose colour and die** when the algae are damaged. This is known as 'bleaching'.

- **Global warming** is the main cause of bleaching. A rise in ocean temperatures interferes with the photosynthetic process, poisoning the algae. Corals expel the dead algae, along with some of their own tissue. Once the algae are expelled, the corals lose their colour and main source of food.

DID YOU KNOW?

Over 50 percent of coral reefs could disappear within the next 40 years as a result of global warming.

▲ *Without the algae that give them colour, corals look white or 'bleached'.*

- **Bleached coral reefs** take years to recover. Bleaching affects not only the coral reefs, but also a large number of marine creatures that depend on them for food.

- **Coral reefs** can also be smothered by silt or sewage draining off the land from buildings operations. If the algae have no light to make food, the corals die.

- **Reefs are often** damaged by heavy anchors from boats used by tourists, or by divers hunting for souvenirs for the tourist trade.

Fragile islands

- **Many threatened species** live on islands, where they are at risk from expanding human populations, global warming and introduced species, such as cats.

- **Island species** are vulnerable because their populations are small and they are often unable to compete with new species that arrive on their island.

- **The dodo bird** lived on Mauritius, an island in the Indian Ocean. It was wiped out by sailors killing it for food, and by introduced species such as rats and monkeys eating its eggs. The last dodo died in 1681.

- **The kakapo** is an almost flightless parrot. Only about 40 live in the wild on two small islands off the coast of New Zealand. All predators have been removed from these islands and human access is controlled.

- **The biggest lizard**, the Komodo dragon, lives on the island of Komodo and a few smaller islands north of Australia. It is threatened by illegal hunting and the spread of human settlements.

- **Lemurs live** on Madagascar, off the coast of Africa. They are threatened by deforestation and also hunted for food and captured for the pet trade or zoos.

▲ *Tourists watching Galápagos sea lions. Tourism has helped to fund conservation projects on the Galápagos Islands, but it could also destroy this fragile ecosystem.*

- **The Galápagos Islands**, off the coast of Ecuador, are home to many rare species, such as giant tortoises, flightless cormorants and Galápagos finches. The growing human population and introduced plants and animals threaten the survival of this unique ecosystem.

Endangered species

- **Endangered species** are animals and plants that are facing extinction. These species will die out if nothing is done to keep them alive.

- **The main reasons** for ocean species becoming endangered are habitat destruction, coastal development and tourism, illegal hunting, overfishing, pollution, climate change, disease, alien or invasive species and increased predation due to changes in the food chain.

- **Endangered ocean animals** include the coelacanth, southern bluefin tuna, leatherback turtle, blue whale, whale shark, great white shark and dugong.

- **All seven species of sawfish** are threatened and the smalltooth sawfish is now endangered. Adult sawfish are hunted for their 'saw' – a long flat snout edged with sharp teeth. Young sawfish are sensitive to coastal development and habitat destruction near the shore.

- **The numbers of baleen whales**, such as right whales and blue whales, were greatly reduced by hunting for their meat and fatty blubber between the 1700s and 1900s. Numbers are still low, even though most commercial hunting is now illegal.

▲ Coelacanths are very rare. It is illegal to trade them and if caught, they should be released back into the wild.

- **The Mediterranean monk seal** is one of the most endangered mammals. There are less than 500 left due to tourism, illegal hunting and pollution. The Caribbean monk seal was declared extinct in June 2008.

- **Dugongs** are close to extinction due to collisions with boats, being accidentally caught in fishing nets and illegal hunting. The seagrass beds where dugongs feed are also being destroyed by dredging, pollution and arm soil being washed into the sea.

- **The deep-water fish** the coelacanth has lived on Earth for about 400 million years, but less than 1000 are probably alive today.

Whales in danger

- **For hundreds of years**, people hunted whales for their meat, bones and blubber. Whale oil was used in lamps and candles and to make margarine, soap, machine oil and cosmetics. Even the baleen was used to make tennis racquets, umbrellas and corsets.

- **At first**, people hunted whales from sailing ships and rowing boats. They killed the whales with spears called harpoons, thrown by hand. The whaling industry expanded after the invention of an exploding harpoon in the 1860s. This could kill even the biggest whales.

- **Commercial whaling** in the 19th and 20th centuries almost wiped out the world's whale populations. Greenpeace estimate that more than 1.5 million whales were killed between 1925 (when the first whaling factory ship was introduced) and 1975.

- **In 1946**, the International Whaling Commission (IWC) was established to try and stop whales from becoming extinct. It regulated the hunting of whales, although it was made up of whaling countries, and whales continued to be killed in large numbers.

- **In 1986**, whale numbers were so low that the IWC banned commercial whaling completely.

DID YOU KNOW?
Seven out of the 13 great whales are still endangered, despite being protected.

▲ Whale bones were used as building materials and tools and to make glue and fertilizer.

- **Today**, some aboriginal peoples still hunt small numbers of whales for food and essential materials. Norway still hunts minke whales in the north Atlantic and Japan kills hundreds of whales (such as minke, Brydes, sperm, fin and sei whales) each year for their controversial scientific research programme.

- **Threats to whales** include noise pollution, climate change, illegal trade in whale meat, entanglement in fishing nets (especially for small whales, such as dolphins), collisions with ships, pollution, habitat degradation and oil and gas exploration.

Turtles in trouble

- **Six out of the seven** types of sea turtle are defined as endangered or critically endangered, including Kemp's ridley, hawksbill, green, leatherback and loggerhead turtles.

- **Several million green turtles** once swam in the oceans, but today less than 200,000 nesting females survive in the wild.

- **Populations of leatherback** turtles have dropped, with numbers estimated at less than 100,000. On one Mexican beach, there were 6500 nests in 1986, but only 50 in 1993.

- **Leatherbacks are killed** for their oil, which is used in lamps and to make ships watertight and also for medicines. These turtles eat a lot of jellyfish and often die after mistaking floating plastic debris for food.

- **Female sea turtles** return to the same nesting beaches each year. They are disturbed by the noise and lights from hotels. Tourists also crush eggs buried in the sand.

- **On some beaches**, nests are protected and people carry the hatchlings to the sea.

▲ *The shell of the hawksbill turtle has been highly prized for thousands of years, and this reptile is now critically endangered.*

- **Poachers may steal** turtles' eggs or cut out the cartilage (calipee) from between the bones of the bottom shell and sell it for making turtle soup.

- **Parts of the shell** of hawksbill turtles are used to make combs, jewellery and spectacle frames.

- **Sea turtles** are an important part of ocean food chains and help to attract ecotourists to tropical beaches. The money raised from tourists supports conservation work and provides employment for coastal communities.

Penguins in peril

- **Four species of penguin** are endangered – Galápagos, yellow-eyed, erect-crested and northern rockhopper penguins. Seven other species face a high risk of extinction and two more are threatened.

- **Emperor penguins** may be seriously threatened in the future due to melting sea ice.

- **Northern rockhopper** penguin populations have declined by about 90 percent in the last 50 years. Scientists think this is probably connected with hunting, climate change, overfishing and wild dogs eating the penguins' eggs.

- **In the past**, people have collected penguin eggs to eat and killed adults for their meat and the oil in their blubber.

- **In 2000**, almost 40 percent of the African penguin population was covered in oil after a tanker sank. Penguins are especially vulnerable to oil pollution on the water's surface as they have to surface to breathe air.

- **African penguin** numbers have declined from 1.5 million breeding pairs 100 years ago to only 63,000 today.

- **Yellow-eyed penguins** of New Zealand are endangered by the destruction of the forests where they nest. Predators such as stoats and ferrets feed on the chicks.

- **Yellow-eyed penguins** also get entangled in fishing nets and drown when they cannot surface to breathe.

- **The Humboldt penguin** is threatened by over-harvesting of the deep piles of guano (penguin droppings) in which they dig their nesting burrows.

▶ *Over the past 45 years, numbers of erect-crested penguins have declined by 50 percent for reasons that are not fully understood.*

The last ice bears

● **Polar bears roam** across the sea ice that covers the Arctic Ocean. They catch seals by waiting next to their breathing holes in the ice and killing the seals when they pop up to breathe.

● **There are about** 20,000 to 25,000 polar bears left in the Arctic but they are in grave danger of extinction.

● **The greatest threat** to polar bears used to be hunting but now they are mainly threatened by global warming, which is causing the sea ice to melt.

● **As the sea ice melts** earlier in summer as a result of global warming, this shortens the winter hunting season for the polar bears. They cannot build up enough fat reserves to last them through the summer when they can't catch seals, and they have to find whatever food is available on land.

● **With less food**, polar bears will not reproduce as often. Their cubs will be smaller and less likely to survive.

● **As well as melting ice**, polar bears are also threatened by poisons in the snow and ice, mining in the Arctic, shipping, tourists, drilling for oil and gas, and illegal hunting or over-hunting for sport.

● **An oil spill in the Arctic** would expose both polar bears and their seal prey to the dangers of oil pollution.

● **Oil exploration and development** could disturb pregnant females choosing a den to give birth to their cubs as well as mothers looking after newborn cubs.

◄ *Global warming is melting the sea ice where the polar bears hunt for ringed and bearded seals.*

Saving the oceans

● **Ocean resources** need to be managed sustainably to avoid destroying habitats, forcing species into extinction and polluting the seas.

● **Less than one percent** of the world's oceans are now marine protected areas (MPAs). Expanding these areas, where fishing, mining and dredging are prohibited, would protect habitats and species.

● **Coastal areas** can be protected by managing the land use based on scientific knowledge so that areas are set aside for different types of activity.

● **The Marine Stewardship Council** (MSC) label provides a way of identifying sustainable fisheries that are not wiping out fish stocks and still allow fishermen to maintain their livelihoods.

● **Many fishing methods** trap and kill other wildlife, such as seabirds and mammals. Different fishing techniques could reduce or avoid this bycatch.

● **To avoid polluting the oceans**, we must reduce the waste we produce, recycle more, control illegal dumping of waste and change dangerous waste into safer waste.

● **Fighting global warming** involves using less energy and developing more sources of alternative energy that do not harm ocean environments.

● **The introduction** of invasive species needs to be avoided as they can disrupt the ocean ecosystem by multiplying rapidly and upsetting the balance of life.

● **Sustainable tourism** is an important part of protecting oceans, coasts and cultures of local people.

◄ *More scientific research into ocean ecosystems and endangered species will help conservation projects to be more effective.*

Index

Entries in **bold** refer to main entries; entries in *italics* refer to illustrations.